Endorsements

Richard J. Foster author of *Celebration of Discipline, Sanctuary of the Soul,* and other books

> All genuine spirituality is local. It is rooted in time and place and people. And in the soil. *Dirt and the Good Life: Stories from Fern Creek* is genuine spirituality. I commend it to you.

Ben Lowe activist and author of *Green Revolution*

> In *Dirt and the Good Life*, the McMinns invite us on their journey as they rediscover what it means to live well and sustainably on God's good earth. Their personal stories and practical reflections radiate beauty and wisdom. We need more authentic and inspiring testimonies like these!

Luke Gascho executive director, Merry Lea Environmental Learning Center of Goshen College and author of *Creation Care: Keepers of the Earth*

> The multilayered vignettes in *Dirt and the Good Life* are inspirational to the soul. Lisa and Mark open up their lives to the reader with poignant reflections on the ways they have engaged with life and land with joy, simplicity, tears and wonder. The personal stories from their small farm, their life experiences and their inner searching are woven together to show the deep meaning of relating to God as the source of life. I heartily resonate with the intentionality of connecting to the earth—the soil—and the meaning that springs from knowing the land and its interconnectedness. Read slowly, reflect deeply, and then put your hands in the dirt!

Tri Robinson author and senior pastor, Vineyard Boise (Idaho)

> There is a deep inner longing in the hearts of many — a longing that I believe God has always intended to be there. It is a longing for what is natural, organic and real. When we touch it we experience a sense of rightness that goes deep, even beyond the understanding that mere cognitive thinking can bring. Lisa and Mark McMinn's personal accounts in their book *Dirt and the Good Life* unravel these truths in such a way that all who read them will be motivated to discover the value of a more sustainable lifestyle.

Steven Bouma-Prediger professor of religion, Hope College, and author of *For the Beauty of the Earth*

> Mark and Lisa McMinn's new book, *Dirt and the Good Life*, is a gem. This collection of 50 short personal meditations, arising from their life together tending their CSA farm in Oregon's Willamette Valley, is insightful, honest, and filled with hope....Read with gusto and enjoy the feast.

Edward R. Brown executive director, Care of Creation; author of *Our Father's World*

> This delightful collection of brief essays offers a glimpse of a "good life" that few of us experience today, and that more of us should look for. In this day of smart phones and 24/7 schedules, I appreciate Mark and Lisa McMinn's reminders of how good it is to reconnect with nature. Not all of us can have the option of packing up and buying a farm in the country, but we can respond to this call by slowing down, taking a deep breath and enjoying God's creation just a bit more. *Dirt and the Good Life* won't tell you how to do it, but this book will certainly make you want to!

Gayle Beebe president, Westmont College;
author of *The Shaping of an Effective Leader*

> *Dirt and the Good Life* is an invitation to human flourishing. The title alone evokes images of Aristotle and his concept of *eudaimonia*—the good life, or more importantly a life governed by human flourishing. Mark and Lisa McMinn's latest book reminds us of values we often glimpse but rarely embrace and invites us to look behind the tapestry of life to celebrate the simple experiences that make life so rich and full. I was especially struck by the invitation to awaken to the rhythms of life, to the sounds of silence that usher in the presence of God, to work, to relationships, to human desire fulfilled in an honorable way, to the deliberate development of an orientation to life filled with meaning and purpose. All these invitations remind us of the richness of a life lived well.

Matthew Sleeth MD, executive director, Blessed Earth;
creation care author and speaker

> God has given us the responsibility of stewardship over His creation. Cultivating the land with respect is one way to gracefully accept this task. In *Dirt and the Good Life*, the McMinns share personal stories of producing their own food, caring for their family and animals, and the peace they have found through farming the land they love. A wonderful read for anyone seeking the Good Life!

Mike Mercer executive director, Northwest Earth Institute

> The McMinn's experience illustrates a rich and full life based on the importance of relationships...to the soil and the planet that sustains us, the moment, loved ones, and our faith.

Fred Bahnson writer and permaculture gardener; co-author with Norman Wirzba of *Making Peace with the Land: God's Call to Reconcile With Creation* (InterVarsity)

For a long while now we Americans have been telling ourselves the wrong story: that dirt is dirty, that food should be cheap, that manual labor is a burden to be shirked. We're all witness to the fallout from that fairy tale, but thankfully people like the McMinns are choosing to live a new story, which is really an old story, the one that says we humans were created from humus, that being human means caring for the humus. In *Dirt and the Good Life*, the McMinn's give us a bushel basket of delightful stories showing how to do just that

DIRT AND THE GOOD LIFE
Stories from Fern Creek

Lisa Graham McMinn
Mark R. McMinn

BARCLAY PRESS
Newberg, Oregon

www.barclaypress.com

DIRT AND THE GOOD LIFE
Stories from Fern Creek

© 2012 by Mark and Lisa McMinn

BARCLAY PRESS
Newberg, OR

www.barclaypress.com

All rights reserved. No part may be reproduced for any commercial purpose by any method without permission in writing from the copyright holder.

PHOTO CREDITS
Photo on page 132 and back cover photo of authors are by Emily Haven,
cover photo and photos on
pages 102, 160, and 165 by Mark McMinn,
all other photos by Lisa McMinn.

COVER DESIGN
BY DARRYL BROWN

ISBN 978-1-59498-026-8

DEDICATION

In memory of our farming grandparents,
John and Anna Schauermann
and
Loyd and Irene Anderson

ACKNOWLEDGMENTS

We like books that emerge out of lived lives and so audaciously decided to write one. Lots of people contributed to *Dirt and the Good Life* because they have influenced and shaped who we've become as farmers, spouses, and simple people living in this nook of the world in the twenty-first century. Some contributors are mere acquaintances: farmers, gardeners, beekeepers, and clerks at Farm and Feed stores that we've consulted in the last five years. Others are lifetime friends and newish ones. Thank you all. You likely know who you are. So to avoid the risk of overlooking some by trying to name others individually, we will mention only a few.

George Fox University granted both of us a sabbatical, and along with some more academic projects we created space for this one. Every Thursday we'd head to Starbucks in McMinnville to write, revise, and critique each other's essays. The pattern wove a rich thread into our sabbatical life that extended throughout the entire year. Dan McCracken, the Publisher of Barclay Press, showed faith in this project from the beginning. We wondered if we had written a narcissistic rant, but Dan believed that people would find meaning, hope, and reasons to laugh as they read our storied life. Paula

Hampton made it better—using her critical eye and careful pen to sharpen and shape as needed. Thank you Paula and Dan for your work and belief.

Finally, since so many of these stories include some dimension of farming—tilling, weeding, planting, harvesting, taking care of bees and chickens—we want to thank all our CSA (Community Supported Agriculture) members for entrusting their food growing to us. They have been enthusiastic supporters of Fern Creek, and by default, of us. They inspire us to grow more and better—both of things that emerge out of dirt and other things that grow out of our souls. Indeed, those two seem more connected these days than we once imagined.

OTHER TITLES BY LISA GRAHAM McMINN

Walking Gently on the Earth
Making Faithful Choices about Food, Energy, Shelter and More
(Inter-Varsity Press)

Sexuality and Holy Longing
Embracing Intimacy in a Broken World
(Jossey-Bass)

The Contented Soul
The Art of Savoring Life
(Inter-Varsity Press)

Growing Strong Daughters
Encouraging Girls to Become All They're Meant to Be
(Baker Books)

OTHER TITLES BY MARK R. McMINN

Sin and Grace in Christian Counseling
An Integrative Paradigm
(Inter-Varsity Press)

Integrative Psychotherapy
Toward a Comprehensive Christian Approach
(Inter-Varsity Press)

Finding Our Way Home
Turning Back to What Matters Most
(Jossey-Bass)

Psychology, Theology, and Spirituality in Christian Counseling
(Tyndale House Publishers)

The Jekyll/Hyde Syndrome
Controlling Inner Conflict Through Authentic Living
(Barclay Press)

Christians in the Crossfire
Guarding Your Mind Against Manipulation and Self-deception
(Barclay Press)

Contents

Introduction	1

CULTIVATING SIMPLICITY

Laundry Day	7
Slumbering Under Stars	11
Out of the Blue	14
The Fitness of Being	17
Downward Mobility	21
Out of the Silence	24
A Good Day's Work	28

CULTIVATING COMMUNITY

Equinox	33
On Birthing Babies and Letting Go	37
Empty Nests and Full Ones	41
Longitudinal Community	44
The Winds of Change	48
The First Annual Pumpkin Carving Extravaganza	52
Silty Clay Rites	56

CULTIVATING COMPASSION AND JUSTICE

Morning (Mourning) Labor	61
Empowering a Maran	66
Tending Dirt	70

Hoeing 74

Sex and Fern Creek 78

Economics 82

Tender Fire 85

CULTIVATING GRATITUDE AND GENEROSITY

Play It Again 89

Choosing Gratitude 92

Becoming an Old Woman (in the West) 96

His and Her Vacation (His) 99

His and Her Vacation (Hers) 102

Surprised by Generosity 107

Valentine's Day 111

Trivia 115

CULTIVATING HOPE

Emptying Out the Locker 119

Saying Grace 122

Strawberry Fields Forever 125

A Call Toward Life 128

Growing Old 132

The Children's Farm 136

Grace in the Kitchen 139

CULTIVATING HUMILITY AND OPENNESS

Apprenticing Life 143
When the Clouds Roll In 146
A Waste of a Worry 149
Being a Man 153
On Dandelions 156
Home Building 160

CULTIVATING FAITH AND INTEGRITY

The Arms of God 165
Finding God in the Pole Beans 169
On Thankfulness for Old Barns and Old Farmers 172
Life and Death 175
Choosing Paths 179
A Magnificat Moment 183
On Preservation 187
On Earth As It Is in Heaven 191

Use the QR code below
or the web address
for additional information about this book
including color versions of the photos
at the beginning of each narrative.

www.barclaypress.com/McMinn

Introduction

John and Anna Schauermann farmed 160 acres in Fort Morgan, Colorado, while Loyd and Irene Anderson tended their 80 acres in Hillside, Oregon. Neither John nor Loyd graduated from high school—or even started. John, a stout German immigrant, came from a long line of farmers and went to the fields out of family habit. Meanwhile, Loyd worked in the sawmill and on the farm to send money to his struggling family in Arkansas. John and Loyd—who never knew one another—each married, tilled the soil, raised crops and children, and then died.

The youngest daughters of each—our mothers—live a mile apart in a small Oregon town and play bridge together each week. Both enjoyed greater economic prosperity than their parents. And the good life for the two of us in the next generation includes PhDs and work as college professors. We have our iPads, an ample three-bedroom house, healthy vitas, and a retirement account. Our children are married and educated and carrying on with whatever remains of the American dream.

We like to hope that if John and Anna, and Loyd and Irene could have looked forward they would have been pleased. Their sweat and tenacity cascaded through three generations. They worked unbelievably hard and now their children, grandchildren, great-grandchildren, and great-great-grandchildren experience the good life. But in the gaining of this life we call good—defined to no small extent by 30-second commercials that fill our airwaves—we may have left behind some of the simple goodness that defined life for our grandparents and parents.

Five years ago we made a life-altering decision that caused us to reconsider the contours of the good life. We were tenured professors at a nationally-recognized liberal arts college: one of us (Mark) in an endowed chair position in the psychology department and the other (Lisa) a department chair of a vigorous, diverse sociology/anthropology department. Our children were launched. We lived in a newly constructed home in the western suburbs of Chicago. Our mortgage was manageable. We had time and money and good friends. Our home theater had Dolby 5.1 surround sound, and the crown molding in our living room was magnificent. What more could we possibly want? *Or what less?*

We walked and talked in the neighborhood or nearby forest preserves almost every evening and again on the weekends. During our many walks we found ourselves talking more and more about heading home. This began as a geographical conversation about moving back to our home state of Oregon. But the conversation continued long after the geographical move concluded, causing us to reconsider what it means to be connected to community, to God, and to the earth.

The year 2006 became a significant marker in an ongoing journey. We took teaching positions at George Fox University, resigned at Wheaton College, sold our Winfield home, and purchased five acres four miles outside of Newberg, Oregon. These were the tangible changes, but the more transformative shift was also occurring.

Our ongoing conversations, starting in Illinois and continuing in Oregon, brought us back to the dirt, to the miracle of new life that must have surely intrigued our grandparents every time they knelt and inspected a newly germinated sugar beet or the blossoms on another year's crop of strawberries or apples. We discover that same miracle as we grow broccoli, lettuce, kale, chard, onions, potatoes, spinach, beets, kohlrabi, apples, pears, squash, beans, carrots, herbs, and berries of various sorts. We identify the parcel of dirt where this happens as Fern Creek. It seems more proper to give this peaceful five acres a name than to call it "our property," which falsely implies that we can claim a part of God's earth as our own. Fern Creek belongs to the squirrels and deer, the bees and the berries they pollinate, the grandchildren who we hope will soon frolic in the forest, the verdant earth that provides us with all sorts of vegetables and fruit to enjoy. Fern Creek is where we often see grace these days, because it is a place of wonder and mystery and adventure. The same dirt that stains the knees of our work jeans ministers deeply to our embodied souls.

Many days—most days, really—we look at one another and simply marvel at how blessed we are by this good life. We are filled with a profound awareness of how good life has become; and more than that, we are seeing how good life has always been, though we have sometimes failed to notice. This does not mean that life has always been easy. Every life is terribly hard sometimes, but glimpses of grace come in the midst of it all just as surely as a God of grace and truth came to dwell in the squalor of human struggle and depravity.

Our life at Fern Creek has become a sanctuary of centered reflection, gratitude, and peace. Perhaps it seems overly bold to say we have finally found the good life—both because our life in Wheaton was very good and because some of our present days are still marked with the quirks and flaws that have always plagued us—but we clearly turned a corner when we sojourned back home.

Our "formative" years came in an era that contrasts significantly from today. We were raised at the tail end of the Baby Boom generation, around the time that Vietnam and Watergate and hippies meandering the country in painted Volkswagen buses shattered societal linearity and certainty. Some might say that modernism began to give way to postmodernism during those years. Perhaps. Whatever happened, listing principles for effective living became more difficult. Back in the days of certainty, we were told a healthy life could be achieved by following a particular set of standards: "Read this book, apply these principles, and your life will be changed forever." Principles and guidelines are fine; but life is undeniably complex, and even lives we label *good* are replete with challenge, pain, and struggle. Wisdom comes more through gentle breezes, or sometimes gusts, than through a list of propositions or principles for effective living.

In the pages that follow we invite you into our storied life, filled with glimpses of grace in everyday moments—laughing with a smiling granddaughter, hiking in the mountains, savoring a chocolate chip cookie, hanging up laundry, weeding, sipping fruit smoothies with friends on a summer evening, noticing a cantaloupe blossom surrounded by honeybees. These may seem like small events, but they are not. These daily moments burst with the largeness of life—the discipline of seeing beauty around us, the conversations of friendship that extend over many years, the materiality of our existence that gives meaning to the Word becoming flesh and dwelling among us.

The wonder of life cannot be fully contained in a solitary self, so we speak of it often to one another—over oatmeal in the morning, while harvesting vegetables in the garden, as we sit on the porch in the evening and reflect on the passing of another day. After speaking of life's goodness day after day for several years now, the time has come to write about it. For us, writing has become a discipline—a spiritual discipline, really—that helps us make sense of life's nuances and complexities. Each day is a gift we need to savor and try to understand as well as two souls can comprehend a thing. We encounter one another amidst the discipline of noticing and experiencing gratitude for all of life. The essays that follow invite you into the same discipline.

If life is storied, then anecdotes and images define the good life better than lists. Christian novelist and theologian Frederick Buechner put it aptly: "If God speaks to us at all in this world, if God speaks anywhere, it is into our personal lives that he speaks" (*The Sacred Journey: A Memoir of Early Days*, San Francisco: HarperSanFrancisco, p. 1). May our lives touch yours in the pages that follow, and may you see glimpses of grace that offer hope, wisdom, and grace.

Mark and Lisa McMinn
Fern Creek
January 2012

CULTIVATING SIMPLICITY

Laundry Day

Every writer knows that words fall short, so Lisa tends to wander Fern Creek with her Canon Rebel in hand, archiving life by photograph. She has a knack for this that I will never have despite her various efforts to teach me about framing and sunlight and texture.

Each year Lisa publishes her favorite photographs in a Fern Creek calendar that becomes a Christmas gift for friends and family. She has many lovely photographs by now, but my all-time favorite is titled "Laundry Day at Fern Creek." In the foreground is a large yellow sunflower, filled so full with seeds that it can hardly stand up straight, and behind it in some artsy, out-of-focus state that only photographers understand, is our outdoor clothesline surrounded by wildflowers and filled so full with damp clothes that it also looks vulnerably crooked. An aging wicker basket sits on the gravel, waiting for the sun-dried laundry.

In addition to its artistic beauty, this photograph blesses me with its simple reminder of the way Lisa chooses to live. I suppose I choose it, too, but some things emerge out of Lisa's passions until I catch the vision.

One of the things I admire about Lisa is her desire to live consistently with her values. She is, by nature, a conservationist. I am, by nature, a bit resistant at first but easily persuaded with time, making me a co-conservationist after 32 years of marriage. We wash out and reuse plastic bags, for example—even ones without the zip-lock thingy. We never throw away a rubber band or a paper clip, because they can be reused. Our computer printer is fed with scratch paper unless we are printing something exceedingly important. We rarely eat meat, in part because growing a pound of vegetables uses fewer of the earth's resources than does growing a pound of meat. Our geothermal heat pump heats and cools our house, saving up to 70 percent of the energy used by traditional heat pumps. A recycled plastic product serves as a very nice deck flooring for our wraparound porch, our indoor floors are bamboo, and, like many in the Portland area, we drive a hybrid car. What we don't conserve, we recycle: paper, plastic, aluminum, glass. We don't even have garbage service at our house, electing instead to take our sparse collection of refuse to the transfer center every few months. Lisa's book title *Walking Gently on the Earth* is a good description of how we try to live.

Most of these conservation efforts come fairly naturally to me by now, but the one that still challenges me most is line drying our clothes. I pull the damp wad of clothes out of the washer, and my hands just automatically stuff the wad into the dryer sitting alongside. That's why we buy a set, right? We get a washer *and* dryer—one washes the clothes, and the other dries them. And they make laundry day so very easy.

Lisa tells me—and I have confirmed this with my online reading—that clothes dryers consume as much as 12 percent of household energy use. When multiplied by the number of households in our country alone, this translates to many boxcars of coal used to fuel our energy companies. Every time I mindlessly toss the laundry from one half of the side-by-side to the other, I contribute to our accelerating depletion of fossil fuels and to climate change.

Lisa takes laundry from the washer, loads it in that old wicker basket, grabs another wicker basket with clothespins, and carries both to the outdoor clothesline where she hangs our laundry—garment by garment. We are quite egalitarian in most of our household chores, but she tends to do the laundry, knowing I will use the electric dryer if I do it. Lisa does this, even though I sometimes play basketball and just generally sweat more and get dirtier than she does, and thus create the majority of our dirty laundry.

One day this summer, shortly after looking at the laundry day photograph again, the power of Lisa's quiet testimony struck me. For almost a decade now she has done my laundry, hanging each pair of socks and underwear, clothespin by clothespin. She does it because she loves me, but also because she loves God and God's good creation. It's the sort of quiet, steady consistency that is woven into Lisa's character, as it was in her father's character before her—a man with an unwavering commitment to daily devotions and studying his Greek New Testament. It made me stop and think.

I want to remain open to changing, to living as simply as possible. Lisa is right about how we ought to dry our laundry; her values are better than mine in this regard. I've been helping with the laundry this summer, clumsily holding blouses and shirts and socks and underwear to the line with one hand as I fumble with clothespins in the other. And I enjoy the warmth from the sunshine that causes sunflowers to grow full and tall around our clothesline and at the same time dries our clothes.

Lisa

Slumbering Under Stars

Sleeping under stars wrapped in warm summer darkness rides near the top of my favorite reasons to backpack. I do less backpacking now that summers are full of farming, but when we built the house we added a small porch off our bedroom that functions well enough as a sleeping porch.

A lawn chair cushion serves as my mattress with my backpacking Therma-Rest mat underneath for an additional inch of padded comfort. I make up my bed and toss the old rainbow quilt I made more than 25 years ago over the top. Scraps of fabric left from dresses I sewed in high school became rainbows and birds and the sight of them can still take me back to those days. I take my pillow (okay—two pillows) and plan to sleep poorly. Mostly the summer Oregon nights turn cold enough that the appeal of my husband's warm and welcoming body draws me back inside. Partly I'm thinking

I'll be less grumpy if I get three to four hours of good sleep, so I usually crawl back into our shared bed around 2:30 or so.

I'm drawn outside by the stars and so sleeping under a new moon is best. I sleep poorly because I can't keep my eyes closed. They constantly pop open to take in the night sky full of stars. I feel deliciously small—one life form on a planet in a tiny solar system that's part of the rather insignificant Milky Way galaxy which gets entirely lost in a sky mostly full of big spaces spotted by galaxies here and there. If we could back up far enough, we could see it the way God can. Yet God, who formed and holds the galaxies, black holes, and star-making nebula, is attentive enough to care what happens in my neck of the woods and to cherish the middle-aged woman sleeping on the porch.

The owl that lives in the barn with the bats lets me know he (she?) is awake, and I hope he will keep hooting for a while yet. This time of night all those bats fly to and fro over the creek and around Fern Creek, eating 1,200 insects every hour. I smile and thank them that my fitful sleep at least is *not* fitful because of the buzzing of mosquitoes looking for exposed skin or a way to sneak under the covers. Bats are our friends—both because we are farmers and they eat insects that eat our vegetables, and because we are people and they eat mosquitoes that eat us. I plan to build a bat house down by the gazebo this winter and hope a few bats take up residence when they return to the barn next spring.

All that to say, God who is big enough to be mindful of an ever expanding universe is small enough to follow the lives of mosquitoes and bats at Fern Creek. The thought of it makes me dizzy and fills me with contentment. I close my eyes until my head stills and eventually I fall asleep. Somewhere around 2:30 when I awake I'll check out the stars once more, listen for the owl, and then haul my weary body and two pillows back to bed where Mark awaits. He will wrap his arm around my cold body, draw me close, and we'll sleep until dawn.

Mark

Out of the Blue

Today we stopped at Lowe's, which Lisa calls "The Blue Store" to distinguish it from "The Orange Store." We wanted some stakes to build a caged-in pathway that would allow our chickens to move freely from their hen house to the garden. November is the magical month when our chickens gain full access to the garden where they chomp away at the summer's waning produce, eat slugs, poop, and scratch in the soil, all the while providing nitrogen, slug control, and aeration for next year's abundance.

Lisa quizzed me on the way: "What store comes to mind when you think of the color red?" (Hint: If your spouse ever asks you this, apparently the correct answer is Target.) "What is the yellow store?" We went through the rainbow, with me failing every question. We eventually parked in the Lowe's parking lot and entered the indoor lumberyard to find our stakes. For $5.72 we could get 24 wooden stakes, but they were 2-foot stakes and we needed 3-foot ones. Looking just beyond the wooden stakes we found a pile of 3-foot metal stakes—lovely, sleek, and sturdy. But they cost $3.71 each, and we needed quite a few of them. So we walked out of Lowe's content to make our own stakes out of scrap wood.

This is our sabbatical year, which gives us large open spaces of time and just a portion of our typical salaries. This year we walk out of Lowe's instead of paying $50 for metal stakes to help guide our chickens' path.

In recent years our life has become financially comfortable. We are rarely extravagant, but we have experienced the freedom to pay the exorbitant cost of popcorn at the movie theater if we so desire, to buy fair-trade chocolate rather than the low-cost varieties that exploit children in West Africa, and to give freely to important causes. We rarely fret about money anymore, but we're experiencing this sabbatical year as a financial adventure that reminds us of how life once was.

During our early-married years we lived on $670 per month. Every dollar was budgeted. Lisa and I did our grocery shopping together—she selected the most cost-effective options and I practiced my mental math so we wouldn't be surprised at the checkout. One day I saw a fellow graduate student buying fresh grapes, and I surged with envy that someone in our same situation would have the resources to buy such a thing. Perhaps she and her husband opted to take out school loans, which Lisa and I chose to struggle along without. I said something silly to Lisa, such as, "Even if we could afford grapes, I hope we wouldn't buy them. They are such an extravagance!" Opinions change with time,

I suppose. We've purchased many grapes—and movie theater popcorn—starting as soon as the financial woes of graduate school ended.

Our sabbatical budget isn't quite as tight as those graduate school budgets, but this year reminds us of the financial caution we exercised back then. We're learning to say no to ourselves again. Our one-click purchases on Amazon.com have dwindled to almost nothing. I canceled my NFL Sunday Ticket subscription, which was outrageously expensive anyway and needed to be canceled. If we buy clothes—a rare occurrence because farmers and college professors tend to be hopelessly out of style anyway—we're as likely to do it at the second hand store as the retail store. We're more intentional and prudent about gift giving and going out for meals. And we make our own stakes instead of buying them at Lowe's.

We do not pretend to understand the challenges of poverty, which can be devastating and overwhelming. This skimpy sabbatical budget is optional because we saved enough to live within our normal budget if we so choose. But Lisa and I don't choose that. Instead, we are enjoying this opportunity to be intentional in living a simpler way of life, to step back to an earlier time and remember the discipline of living sparingly.

Meanwhile, as we walked out of the "blue store" knowing the stockholders would do just fine without us purchasing the metal stakes. The chickens will find their way from the hen house to the garden with our homemade ones. And we will remember the discipline of using money wisely.

Lisa

The Fitness of Being

I learned a new buzzword this week: *functional fitness*. Being functionally fit means that you can reach up to the top shelf in the garage and pull down the box of canning jars without having them tumble on your head (though from personal experience I'd recommend storing them lower down). I suppose the alternative is *non-functional fitness*, which could mean you look buff on the beach but have no practical strength in the home or on the farm.

Hearing about functional fitness made me feel better about my lack of regular gym workouts in the last few years. This morning Mark lamented that he never "worked out" anymore, as in lifting weights in a gym. Yet just this week he loaded and carried 2,800 pounds of bagged concrete that we used to pour the foundation for the fire pit/gazebo we're building down by the creek. When I reminded him, he figured that, okay, maybe he did adequately exercise today. Besides, he was still playing basketball a couple times a week when the farming chores allowed him some breathing space in the middle of the day.

By nature farmers are a functionally fit sort of folk—at least the old world farmers who still use human energy to move dirt and deal with weeds and slugs. New world farmers mostly use petroleum-powered machines to till, plant seeds, and apply pesticides which control undesirable insects and plants that make it difficult to grow food. Old world farmers are found on small family farms. They are the kind we aspire to be. Besides, except for our very small tractor, we can't afford all that fancy machinery.

Last week Mark and I dug 15 holes for footings we poured this week for the gazebo and the footbridge, dealing at times with tree roots or sludge from the creek. The week before I spent several hours yanking out invasive blackberry vines so we could see if the spot I envisioned for the gazebo would be level enough. Wearing my rubber boots, I've been in the creek cleaning it out which involved heaving old bricks, tires, and paint cans up on the bank. A few different muscles definitely were trained with that task, especially when I add hauling everything up the hill so we could take the tires and cans to the dump and line the front grass lawn with the bricks.

Mark's functional fitness involves the heaviest work. Besides hauling bags of concrete to the gazebo site, he does just about all the hauling of lumber, roofing materials, and tools to wherever we're constructing or working. Mark insists it is easier to carry heavy stuff by himself rather than let me help him. Women, I've decided, are generally better at sharing loads. When Megan Anna and I carried a load of lumber to the hen house site, we each grabbed an end and found a way to walk cooperatively. Mark shakes his head in apparent befuddlement.

Our summer fitness routine involves weeding and harvesting (lots of bending over and lifting weights—especially in August and September with so many pounds of beans, cucumbers, squash, pumpkins, and apples that even the chickens grow weary of them). I round out my fitness routine with cleaning out the hen house—emptying and refilling their two-gallon water bucket—and bee tending (usually not too strenuous except when harvesting 50 pound honey supers or lifting brood boxes each week in the spring and early summer to look for larvae, pollen, and honey stores). Beyond that, we nearly always walk the farm, including late afternoon treks down to the hammock by the creek for a rest and a chance to revisit the day.

So when we do take a day off to kayak down the Willamette River, we find loading the kayaks into the pickup truck and carrying them down to the river doesn't seem all that strenuous. Neither does rowing. And when I go out to the garage to get something stored on the shelves Mark put in, I can still climb up onto the pickup truck, teeter on the side wall of the bed to wrestle down a box (or, most recently, my very light Therma-Rest pad, which lay under a stack of not-so-light backpacks). Our farming life appears to be a rather simple, ordinary-life-lived-out way of keeping both of us functionally fit, which is, after all, a sweet gift we give each other. I hope we'll still be functionally fit another 20 years from now.

Does it seem paradoxical that most of us who work out (including me for about 15 years) do so by driving to an air-conditioned gym where we use more fossil fuel to run on a treadmill and where we use weight machines to "train" our muscles so that we can go sit behind a desk at work? I'm not knocking fitness. I'm obviously a big fan of using one's body—pushing it beyond what we think it can do and keeping it fit, flexible, and healthy. But I wonder what our exercise routines say about our place in history—that a typical middle-class life is so sedentary we have to work out in gyms to maintain some level of fitness. The fact that we've only recently decided to work toward *functional* fitness perhaps highlights how very sedentary our complex lives have become.

Mark

Downward Mobility

In 2004 I wrote a book that changed the course of my life, but more because of its failure than its success. A couple of publishers bid for it. I ultimately decided to go with the one that offered what seemed to me a huge advance, and we discussed a big, elaborate marketing plan. When they got the manuscript, they told me it read like a Philip Yancey book, and I began letting my imagination run away with me. An excerpt was published in *Christianity Today* as the book was being released, and it was named a finalist in the Gold Medallion book award competition. The publisher chose a questionable title and put on an orange cover that looked like fire and brimstone. It may have been the title or the cover, or maybe the marketing conversations were forgotten. Maybe the book just wasn't as good as I thought it was. For whatever reason, the book utterly flopped, like one of those painful belly flops we all experience as kids (hopefully only once). I received the out-of-print letter within a year of the book's release.

The failure of that book, I now realize, was God's grace. It caused me to stop and assess the flow of my life. I realized how self-absorbed I had become, and how much my entire career had been pointed toward the home run that I now realize I will never hit. It was a wake up call, a chance to reprioritize and to consider what Henri Nouwen calls *downward mobility*. I still enjoy writing, but in a strange way this event shifted my priorities so that now one of the greatest joys of life comes from working in the dirt. A friend saw the 100-foot irrigation trench I dug by hand last year and seemed genuinely worried that I might be losing my mind. Upward mobility has its place, but so does downward mobility. And there is nothing quite so good as working in the dirt to remind us where we come from and where we are headed.

Life at Fern Creek produces little notoriety or financial return. Our trips to the airport have become less frequent as have invitations to speak, and my aspirations to write a bestseller have greatly receded.

One more thing should be said. Lisa and I are happier, and more content and grateful, than we have ever been. Life is so very good, filled with simple pleasures. We smile more, and laugh, too. Who could have known how good homemade tomato sauce would taste during winter months? How could we have imagined the thrill of opening a honeybee colony to inspect it for new brood? What possibly accounts for the deep sighs of contentment that we both release at the beginning and end of almost every day?

Upward mobility has its place in life. We climb through educational levels, strive to maximize our earning potential,

Mark

Out of the Silence

Growing up on a hazelnut and walnut farm in Northwest Oregon, I learned early about open places and the vastness of silence. Many of my high school days were spent walking through the orchard cutting suckers from the hazelnut trunks, weeding out nature's competition so that the trees could grow straight and strong. Apart from a tractor in a distant field or an occasional plane passing by overhead, those days were spent in silence. I suppose I could have found an AM/FM transistor radio with an earphone to distract me, but I didn't.

College was a shock for me, moving from a quiet 45-acre farm to an urban campus bustling with activity and sounds of all sorts. Stereos blared the 70s sounds we stored on 8-track tapes, people chattered all hours of the day and night, traffic hummed, Walkmans were born. Still, I pursued rise to positions of influence. All this makes for potentially meaningful contributions and is worthy of notice and celebration. But it all must end eventually, because what goes up must come down.

We are in the process of growing old, Lisa and I, and every aging soul must eventually face the question of changing the world. We tried. I'd like to hope we did some good along the way, encouraging and inspiring the next generation. They often imagine they will change the world, too. Maybe we do change the world some, but not nearly as much as I imagined as a young man, and maybe we change the world more through our kindnesses to one another than through grand accomplishments. It is both expected and good that we try to climb higher, to do something bigger and better before we die, but too often this devolves into clamoring, empire-building, grasping. At some point—whether 30 minutes or 30 years before death—we must accept the inevitability of our downward descent. If we are intentional, downward mobility moves us to a place of quiet pondering—to the center, to peace, contentment, and gratitude for the gift of life.

Lisa and I are part of a Quaker church, which involves worship in the tradition of Friends. Each week we spend part of the service in silence—and not with a piano playing in the background. This is deep, prolonged silence, terrifying to some and profoundly meaningful to us. Silence allows space to practice letting go as we hush the clamor of our ambitions long enough to sink down into centered quiet. There, in the stillness, where knowing God and knowing self come together, where peace and contentment take their rightful place, we find the grace to follow God's leading, whether upward or downward.

the noise of life off the farm. First a bachelors degree, then a doctorate, my first academic job, my first book (then another), three daughters to raise, a private practice to build, talks to give. Noisy as it was, life kept coming at me, and I loved it. I never imagined going back to the farm.

Discovering the Friends (Quaker) church was like coming home. Silence, or open worship, is traditionally a part of every Friends service. Open worship occurs amidst the silence, but it is more than silence. We discipline ourselves to listen—to the inner rhythms of life, to the nudging of God, and to one another when someone in the community stands to speak. There is silence to be sure, but the listening that comes out of the silence is the greater treasure. In some Friends meetings, open worship is the sole agenda; in others it is one part of a programmed meeting.

Roman Catholics practice the beauty of contemplative silence as well. When Lisa and I lived in Illinois and couldn't find a Friends church, we worshipped at a nearby Protestant church and also found the Cenacle Retreat Center, run by the Cenacle Sisters, where we could go each Monday evening for a contemplative service of silence. Sunday brought lively praise choruses from a worship band, which we enjoyed and found spiritually meaningful; Monday brought the solace and fullness of silence, which ushered us into the presence of God.

I wonder how often we misperceive silence to be absence, or even nothingness. We imagine that silence occurs when the podcasts run out or the batteries expire on the latest electronic device. Silence, we think, is like an empty gas tank—something that needs to be filled at the next possible opportunity.

What if we have it backward?

Maybe silence is fullness—the capacity to listen to God amidst all life offers, the sum of everything that has ever been and everything to come. Perhaps silence is presence, listening—God with us here and now in this moment and every moment that has come before, speaking quietly into our lives of hurry.

Working in Fern Creek's dirt brings its share of silence, reminding me of the childhood farm that I once felt happy to leave. I spend hours hoeing and harvesting, much of it solitary work. The dirt we farm is a silent sort of community replete with minerals and tiny critters. Like silence, dirt is not emptiness or nothingness, but fullness and abundance. Out of dirt's silence comes life, a reminder of God's sustaining presence in this noisy world.

As with finding fellowship among Quakers, working in the dirt feels like coming home.

Working in this dirt helps me hear the inner clamor. I so readily fill up my experience with words, drowning out God's still small voice with my daily "to do" list or in preparing my next talk. Sometimes I rehearse petty grievances in my mind and only later recognize how I have squandered my time of silence with vapid inner conversation that ought not be voiced. But other times, in sweet days of centeredness, I become attentive to the fullness of silence, evident in the dirt beneath my feet. As my fingers move through soil I participate in the history of this land that has nourished trees and cattle and grasses of various kinds. I notice the here-and-now: earthworms and beetles, ladybugs and fungi. I help shape the future of what will grow in my generation and the next. Material meets immaterial, and my ensouled body (or is it an embodied soul?) finds the deep joy God created me to know.

All sorts of fruits and vegetables grow up out of this silent dirt world, bearing witness to an abundant life that needs no decibels to thrive. Here, amidst the quiet, God is.

Lisa

A Good Day's Work

Yesterday Tami came out to farm with us on Fern Creek. In addition to Jacob, who we've hired to help us ten hours a week, Tami and Ed come volunteer occasionally. They're souls who delight in digging in dirt and hanging out with small-scale farmers, tomato vines, and swarming bees.

Tami, Ed, and Jacob want to understand the habits of chickens, to know when to harvest honey from the hives (and how to do it), and how—without the use of pesticides—to keep slugs and beetles from consuming broccoli and lettuce. They appreciate the crisp goodness of a snap pea straight off the vine or the red burst of sweet from a strawberry sunning in the field. Because Jacob is here on a regular basis, he is getting the broadest education. In addition to learning what it takes to grow food naturally, he learns how two married people work out their differences when it comes to harvesting potatoes or scheduling irrigation. He has helped Mark with electrical work and carpentry, and next week he will participate in the slaughter and subsequent de-feathering, cleaning, and butchering of one of our hens. He's been up for any experience we've tossed his way, even the clandestine one that included tagging along on a salvaging expedition.

We like to send those who help us farm home with a gift from Fern Creek's abundance: lettuce, eggs, early potatoes, or at least some "Grade B" produce that, nibbled too much by other critters, can't be given to our Community Supported Agriculture (CSA) families. Still, it's produce we all agree is good enough to eat. The chickens get "Grade C" produce, and the compost pile receives anything left over.

A few weeks ago Jacob redeemed some strawberry runners we'd tossed out into the meadow and had taken root there, and I've sent him home with runt basil, pepper, and tomato plants. He bikes out to Fern Creek from town and manages to get plants home and in the dirt with very little stalk and leaf damage from the transition. Yesterday after he and Mark thinned the corn patch, I walked by his open backpack and saw he'd stuck a few corn plants into a plastic bag. He's got a junior Fern Creek farm growing in Newberg and my soul smiles big at the thought.

Yesterday Tami harvested lettuce with me, and broccoli, chard, rosemary, and thyme. We washed the onions and potatoes Mark and Jacob harvested and she helped me put the crates together for our CSA families—people who make the weekly trek out to Fern Creek for 18 weeks in the growing season to pick up whatever food is ripe and ready. They pay us up front to be their farmers, putting faith in our ability to grow vegetables and fruits and trusting our promise to do it naturally—that is, in ways that do not harm the dirt, beneficial insects, or ultimately our subscribers. When our subscribers come out, we invite them to stroll or tromp in the woods, feed the chickens scratch (or Grade C produce), or sit in the chairs by the hives to watch the bees go about the business of collecting nectar and pollen. Some bring a picnic lunch. Our youngest member comes with his mother, a Moby-wrapped bundle nestled into his mama's body; our oldest member lives in a retirement community.

Our Fern Creek community reminds me that we're doing important work—growing food that feeds families. Beyond that we are giving people the opportunity to connect again to the seasonal food cycles of our ancestors, to note more directly the work required to produce food, and to remember that actual bees, chickens, and people are behind the honey, eggs, vegetables, and fruit they eat.

While Tami and I put the crates together, Jacob and Mark hoed onions, mounded the potatoes, and planted fall cabbage. When Mark made a burrito run to town (something we do as a celebratory lunch break from our labor every now and then), Tami and Jacob cut and clipped up the tomato vines while I put the finishing touches on the weekly newsletter (with its tips and recipes) that I include in the crates each week.

We ate lunch on the picnic table out back and suddenly it occurred to me: *this* picture of farming captured my longings. A few souls working together—some older and wiser in the realms of farming, some younger and stronger with their futures before them—all of us learning together and valuing each other's contribution and presence. Later Mark and I took our afternoon break in the hammock down by the creek and reflected on a good day's work. We lay down head to feet so we can look at each other as we nap or talk.

Mark tends to nap; I tend to talk. Often simultaneously. Or when Mark naps, I listen to the squirrels and various birds and the constant play of water as it falls from the culvert onto the rocks and into the creek bed below.

I looked at the dirt under my fingernails—the mark of my very dirty life from March through October—and smiled.

CULTIVATING COMMUNITY

Mark

Equinox

Many years ago, when Lisa and I lived in a 1970s-style home on Cedar Street, she suggested I build a gazebo in the back yard. "What's a gazebo?" I asked. If truth be told, I actually accused her of making up the word. This was long before Google searches on the Internet, so it took her a while to convince me otherwise. I built something that may have roughly resembled a gazebo-like structure, but it looked more like a storage shed with a deck on top. It sounds strange because it was strange.

This summer, almost 30 years later, I built a real gazebo with Lisa's help. It has six sides, a fire pit in the middle, cedar benches, a shelf for marshmallow skewers, and a shake roof. I figure every home construction hobbyist should install a shake roof once—and only once—in his lifetime. Lisa and I finished our gazebo in time for our fall equinox party which always involves a campfire and the possibility of s'mores. I find the possibility of s'mores more gratifying than the sticky, sugary reality of the things. But then again, chocolate is timeless.

Five years ago Lisa came up with the idea of celebrating seasonal shifts. "Let's have a fall equinox party," she said.

"What's an equinox?"

Even after Lisa's explanation I remained unclear why we would want to celebrate such a thing. But celebrate we have, year after year, and I must admit it has been great.

On or near September 21 we bring friends together for a seasonal meal, mostly from our soon-to-fade summer gardens. Then we sit around the campfire and share poems or memories or stories about autumn. Someone almost always reads a Wendell Berry poem and a children's story, and inevitably someone mentions the beginning of football season. This year we talked about the school supply list we enjoyed during elementary school years and the types of lunch pails we carried to school. We laugh, and sometimes sing, and reflect on changing seasons in life. After the darkness falls and the fire expires, we stumble through the woods back to the warm house where we all agree what a wonderful time we have enjoyed. As goodbyes are said to one another for the evening, we recognize that we are also saying goodbye to summer for another year. But neither of these are sad goodbyes because we have built a good memory with our friends while welcoming the splendor of another autumn.

This year our sabbatical schedule allowed us to spend most of the day preparing a garden feast before our guests arrived at 6 p.m. We made a marinara sauce with fresh tomatoes, onions, oregano, and thyme from the gardens, chopping and stirring and stewing our way to a farm fresh topping for whole grain penne. Lisa sliced and roasted more tomatoes, adding just the right amount of balsamic vinegar and mixing in some red onion and basil. I took her concoction and put it atop some toasted Italian bread for what became amazing bruschetta. Lisa made an eggplant gratin, which takes way more time than eggplant deserves. I hear it was marvelous (I mostly avoid eggplant). Then we chopped and roasted various vegetables—onions, beets, carrots, delicata squash, and summer squash. We picked and cut fresh apples for an apple cranberry crisp. It was a full day in the kitchen for sure. But when all the food came together and our friends did too (along with some falafel-chip-with-hummus appetizers and an Oregon pinot noir) it was an incredible time together. We ate great food, shared laughter and stories and reflections of fall, enjoyed a fire in the new gazebo, and eventually said goodbye to summer and one another.

Our equinox party reminds us how friends walk with us through changing seasons and passing of time. John and Cindy have been casual friends for 27 years now, though we rarely talked during our 13 years in the Midwest. But when John almost died from *E Coli* poisoning, we prayed earnestly every day despite our geographical distance. Every time I see John I remember God's healing and restoring presence in creation. Scott and Diana were students of mine a couple of decades ago, and Scott's father once worked with my father many years ago. Scott and Diana were the first to have us to their house for dinner when we moved back to Oregon. They are fine people we would like to get to know better. Paul and Janette live a few farms over. I recall gathering in their living room a few years back, praying for Janette amidst her frightening cancer diagnosis. She is surviving as well as an embodied soul can survive, always quick to smile and ready to help others out. Dana and LaNeal participate in our monthly reading group. They are amazing parents, inspiring in the virtuous life they live, and are becoming good friends. Each year we bring together a different group of friends, which reminds us how our paths cross, and crisscross, over years. The equinox campfire causes us to slow down enough to remember.

Days slip by so fast, and weeks and months, seasons and years. I love that Lisa wanted to start marking these seasons with equinox and solstice gatherings. They cause us to stop and be intentional about these fleeting days of life, to "waste" incredible amounts of time in the kitchen so that we can remember God's lavish grace so evident in the food that grows from the earth, in the leaves that paint the landscape before falling from their trees, and in the company of friends.

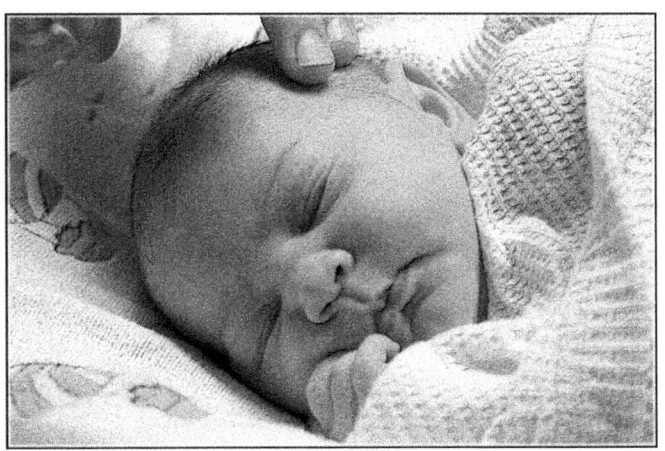

On Birthing Babies and Letting Go

Our daughter, Rae, asked if I would be her birth doula and the request blessed me deeply. She wanted me present to bear witness to, and offer emotional assistance as she did the work of birthing Juniper Rae.

Rae and her sister, Sarah, came out for the afternoon to visit their other sister, Megan Anna, and three-week-old Auden. Later that evening after returning to Portland, Rae called and said her water broke. I wrestled out of bed and drove into Portland on a clear, starlit June 30 night. We thought Juniper Rae would likely be born July 1, but Rae followed my own firstborn birthing pattern and Juniper arrived July 2 after a long labor and a hard birth.

Aubry, Rae, and I wept from both joy and relief when Juniper Rae finally finished her birth journey to begin her longer sojourn on earth. My first post-birth memory—both in my mind and captured on my camera—is my daughter holding my granddaughter. This is followed closely by my memory of Aubry holding Juniper close to his chest with newfound love in his eyes.

Birthing is a giving up, a necessary process of letting go so a child can begin to live. The Western mind makes much of this need to release our children, to let them differentiate—to become autonomous, independent, and capable of making self-determining choices. The Eastern mind sees an infant as already inclined to stretch toward self-determination and so instead seeks to bind infants to the family and to cultural values and norms that give the child identity and a willingness to put needs of family above individual desires.

This is over-simplified, and there is truth in both worldviews. But since my view has been influenced by the West, I value the challenge of an Eastern critique on notions of self-determination. By taking our children to church (or not taking them to church), we are choosing faith (or non-faith) for them. Yes, at some point they may un-choose what we have chosen, but we make the initial determination. If we make mud-pies with them in the dirt, read to them, feed them a vegetarian diet or a meat diet or one low or high in sugar (or broccoli!), we are imparting values, habits, and tastes that will shape them long after they leave home. Even though we think children should be self-determining, we'd never suggest parents should refrain from imparting values and traditions to their children.

We make other significant choices for our children as well. By living near and engaging extended family or living away and knowing extended family mostly through Skype or Facebook, we influence how they think about the role, place, benefits, and obligations of extended family. By moving from one state to another—as we did when our daughters were eight, ten, and twelve—we affect their opportunities, taking away some and giving others, shaping their future significantly by our choices.

Sociologists tend to think it is a myth to believe that our children end up where and who they are because of self-determining choices. They are who they are because of where and when they were born and to whom. All of us are who we are because our parents moved around a lot, or didn't; or farmed, or taught, or worked as clerks, managers, or janitors. We, and our children after us, are formed through our commitments and relationships. We shape each other and so become, and are ever becoming.

Little Junie is now a year old. She and her cousin Auden share similarities and have unique traits that distinguish them. Both are happy babies who smile and laugh easily and are delighted by visits to the hen houses and by Grandpa's elephant sound. A deep ache of gratitude settles in my soul when I think how blessed we are to live near them. I will know them, they will know me, and we will shape each other in the knowing over the years.

Rae released Junie first in birth and will release her in numerous ways through the years to come even as she holds her close, shaping and forming her values, tastes, and habits. In the West when our children turn 18 they are no longer legally bound to us nor us to them, and the strength of the binding we crafted up to then is tested. But perhaps the biggest release is when our daughters and sons become mothers and fathers themselves, when their primary focus shifts to their own children and family. We hold them still, and yet also let them go, finding new ways to graciously support them as they raise the next generation.

Mark

Empty Nests and Full Ones

We've been fighting for spring in Oregon this year, with rainy 40-something-degree days trying to hold off the occasional sun sightings, and doing so quite successfully. I do my daily weather.com browsing, complaining to Lisa about how many degrees below average we will be today while inwardly groaning for the broccoli, cabbage, lettuce, peas, and strawberries that are trying to survive this prolonged cold. Last week the cold subsided for a day, allowing sun to warm the wet earth and reminding us that sunshine always wins eventually.

Lisa and I try to walk rain or shine, but shine is better. As we walked up Rainbow Lane with afternoon rays filtering through the dense evergreen canopy, Lisa spotted and pointed out a bird nest high up in a maple tree—more evidence that spring is on its way. It got me thinking about nest metaphors, empty and full, and the joy we have experienced in raising children.

The full-nested years brimmed with activity: attending school open houses, playing basketball in the backyard, hours of taxiing so familiar to suburban parents, dinner preparations and conversations, praying together before bed, negotiating dating and sibling conflict and who gets to wear clothes belonging to whom. We had stressful and fearful moments, as parents do, but still we reflect gratefully on the great blessing of those years and the privilege of parenting.

The night before our oldest daughter left for college, we gathered in our living room to ponder life's changes and adventures, and I found myself inexplicably overcome with emotion. Sending off a child is no easy thing, though I didn't anticipate how powerfully these feelings might wash over me. Lisa felt them, too, I know, but gracefully managed hers as I shed my tears and we wished Rae God's deep blessings in college and beyond.

In all, we sent three children off.

The empty nest is difficult for some couples, but for us it was the sending off that felt difficult. Once empty, the nest began to feel spacious. We suddenly had time for long evening walks, creativity, and dreaming about the future. One of those dreams gestated into a move back home to Oregon, to live this life at Fern Creek that delights us every day. Lisa and I still marvel at our freedom, in ample amounts of time to pursue our passions, in our life together.

But the empty nest fails as metaphor because our daughters and their husbands still enjoy coming around and filling our lives with good conversation, community, and laughter. The day following our nest-spotting on Rainbow Lane brought Easter, and with Easter came a family dinner at Fern Creek. Each of our three children, their husbands and children, my sister and her daughter, Lisa's mother and mine, and a friend of one of our children gathered at Fern Creek for the afternoon and evening. I learned about a new iPad app called "Words with Friends" from my niece while others played a "real" game of Scrabble in the nook. My son-in-law Luke and I hid chocolate eggs, and plastic eggs filled with jelly beans or quarters. During a delightfully sunny break in the rain, others searched. Four generations of souls frolicked at Fern Creek, reminding us how life carries its blessings through bearing, adopting, and rearing children; saying hello and goodbye countless times; welcoming each season of life as a gift.

Our children were young once. Lisa and I faced all the challenges youthful parents face—managing children who cry at night, distributing diaper changing and household chores, and balancing career with family. It always strikes me as unfortunate that the greatest pressures of life—parenting, finances, education, career-building—seem to reach a simultaneous climax in a single stressful decade of young adulthood. We see our children entering that season, and we pray for their strength and resilience, for enough hope and laughter to balance all the heavy responsibilities they face. Meanwhile we revel in the flexibility that aging brings and in this small multigenerational community that we are privileged to call family.

Mark

Longitudinal Community

Dirt gets a bad rap. "Go outside, but don't get dirty," we say. Or, "Oh yuck, I just got dirt all over my shirt." We even call expletive words *dirty*, as if dirt is as crude as we can be. But dirt tells a story of life. Without dirt and its teeming microbes, fungi, bacteria, amoebas, mites, and earthworms, we perish. People who know claim that the living organisms in one shovel full of dirt outnumber all humans ever born. One might even view dirt as a sort of community of organisms that sustain one another, and ultimately all of creation. In dirt we see a glimpse of God's intelligence and sustaining grace.

Lisa and I spend a lot of time in the dirt these days. We hoe it, till it, fertilize it, inspect it, water it, plant in it. We even watch movies and read about dirt whenever we have opportunity, though we have not yet started eating it as John does in *The Real Dirt on Farmer John*.

Bivocational as we are, my hours in the dirt are interspersed with trips to the computer to check and respond to e-mails, many of them related to doctoral dissertations. As a professor in a doctoral program, I find dissertation supervision both exhilarating and relentless. In working with students on research design, we often discuss cross-sectional and longitudinal research. Cross-sectional looks at data collected from multiple individuals at a certain point in time whereas longitudinal studies look at people over an extended period of time. Then I take these research conversations back outside to the dirt with me where I contemplate the contours of life beyond psychology dissertations.

It occurs to me that dirt's story is really a story of longitudinal community. Most often we think of community cross-sectionally—a group of people we know and love right now at this moment of existence. But communities are also longitudinal. Fern Creek began before us, streaming down through today, into our children, our children's children, and on and on. One of the constants through this longitudinal community is dirt, telling the story of generations past just as surely as it will visit generations to come. The cattle that came before us tromped down the soil and munched the pasture grass that still wants to pop up in our gardens like invasive weeds. They also fertilized the land with their cow pies, unwittingly contributing to the size of our cabbage once we loosen the compressed soil and rid it of grass.

We choose to use natural methods for pest control, such as insecticidal soaps and bacillus thuringiensis, avoiding synthetic pesticides. Partly this is a choice for us, for our CSA subscribers, and for the billions of organisms now living in the dirt. Partly it is choice for those who come after us. We do the same with fertilizer, mixing our concoction of cottonseed meal, kelp, bone meal, and lime rather than resorting to premixed, high-nitrogen synthetic fertilizers. Agricultural scientists disagree about synthetic pesticides and fertilizers and how long they disturb the natural balance of dirt, but all agree these synthetic chemicals have at least short-term effects on microbial life. How we make our broccoli thrive today may impact the corn grown in the next generation and will almost certainly affect the tomatoes we grow next year and the Brussels sprouts the year after.

Arrogance is a folly that visits every generation, but I sometimes wonder if our postmodern perspectives make us all the more vulnerable to it. We suppose that all truth needs to be reconstructed, discovered anew. "What's past is past," we say. "Who knows what the future will hold?" In these adages we express the bliss of ignoring longitudinal community—and our arrogance. The past has surely shaped the present, as the present shapes tomorrow. It is good and lovely to care for our brothers and sisters, our neighbors and neighborhoods, to pursue peace and justice here and now. Yet through it all runs another community—a perpendicular dimension that spans years, and sometimes generations.

For us, Fern Creek is a place of redemption. It is where we have discovered the abundance of whole life that awaits the willing soul. The quiet hours of working in the dirt provide time for renewal and reflection on the big matters of living and dying, time and eternity. And through it all runs a community of those who have come before us—sweating, crying, laughing, tilling, planting, growing, doing the best they can to find the abundant life. The little Douglas Fir trees we planted four years ago will someday loom large over the soil,

Lisa

The Winds of Change

Mark and I planned a quick trip to the Redwood National Forest before our CSA (Community Supported Agriculture) got underway in June. We stayed at the Historic Requa Inn, situated in the heart of the forest and owned and operated by a family—members of the Yurok Tribe—on whose land the inn sits. Something about that makes me want to be extra respectful and attentive.

    I hadn't yet hit puberty the last time I walked in the redwoods. Mom and Dad drove us there from Arizona for a summer vacation—I imagine we were on our way up to Oregon to visit Granny and Granddad, which we did during the summers Dad was home. A lot of summers the Air Force sent him on temporary duty somewhere, and during those years Mom drove us out to Colorado to visit Grandma and Aunt Gerry, Uncle Bill, and our four cousins who lived on living both above the dirt and in it, housing more squirrels and chipmunks than we imagine, helping another generation experience the good gifts that spring forth from dirt.

and farmed the family farm. I loved those vacations most of all. I remember the barn smells, churning butter, helping Uncle Bill set irrigation pipes, watching the migrant workers hoe weeds in the sugar beet field, and riding Ginger (the family horse) who was partly mine because I belonged to Grandma and that meant I partly belonged to the farm. Sometimes we'd go with our cousins to a 4-H event, and once we went to a rodeo, and way more than once I wished their life was mine.

I don't remember many particulars of the childhood redwoods visit, but I remember a Kodak moment captured and now held in one of our family albums. Shades of black, white, and gray show our family encircling a tree, our bodies smashed up against the trunk, arms spread wide, fingers touching, trying to see how far around the tree that Dad, my siblings, and I could reach (while Mom snapped the photo). I remember feeling the bark on my face and, although I may be imagining it now, the utter aliveness of that tree—a tree taller than the Empire State Building and already all grown up before Christopher Columbus lost his way and accidentally set foot in the Americas.

Now, as Mark and I walked through the forest, it occurred to me that little seemed to have changed in the 40 years I'd been away. I find that immeasurably comforting.

I've witnessed a fair bit of change in my lifetime, like the melting of our polar icecaps and the disappearance (and recent reappearance) of family farms. I witnessed the dissolving of the Soviet Union into independent states (our national enemy and presumably the reason the Air Force sent my father away for extended periods of time) and the emergence of a new war on global terrorists. I've seen computers become an essential household appliance (along with cell phones and microwaves) and a cancer epidemic linked by some to environmental changes and our exposure to new carcinogens, like the radiation from our cell phones. The Internet shrank the world. We can get news almost instantly and have access to information and each other anywhere, anytime.

But I digress, as thoughts often do on six-mile hikes through forests. So much change, I thought, yet the redwoods remained largely unchanged by human activity and noise. The redwoods stay as I remembered them from my childhood mostly because of a few forward-thinking people who fought to preserve some of our forests for future generations—to protect them from the desire to consume the trees and develop the land.

We could see that a fire had burned through not too many years ago, yet sword and maidenhair ferns, trillium, daisies, columbine, skunk cabbage, and hundreds of plants that I couldn't name flourished. It's not that nothing had *happened* in the forest. Some trees had fallen, others sprouted; paths had been made and maintained, benches placed; and generations of elk, bear, hawk, and mountain lion had come and gone. And people, too. Perhaps that's what overwhelmed me the most—knowing that people very different from me had lived, loved, and died in these woods at some point, yet also people not so different from me. We all had hopes for our children and ourselves. We all desired peace, a good night's sleep, food, companionship, a place to call home.

Maybe this strong sense of peace I have when I'm in the woods—either the redwoods or the much smaller forest at Fern Creek—is because I best find my place in some big, unchanging, and rather simple picture. I resonate with what I suspect are the hopes of ordinary women and men in every time and place, and I desire to live faithfully and preserve what has been preserved for me. I want to have lived well and pass on a way of life that will bring peace, well-being, and a sense of belonging for the children to come.

Lisa

The First Annual Pumpkin Carving Extravaganza

I'm a sucker for holidays. From mid-October through January 1 I'm giddy in an unreasonable sort of way. I pull out the ceramic pumpkins from the fall decorations box, bring in leaves and gourds, cut down corn stalks, and create fall *displays* (a word that can be said quite disparagingly, it turns out.) Not until early January will I stop arranging and adjusting displays to represent our movement through Halloween, Thanksgiving, the winter solstice, and Christmas.

In October Mark starts lighting fires in the woodstove and I start burning cinnamon, pumpkin, and apple spice candles. Mark knows I get a bit wacky once the cold and rain of fall settles in. I'll start figuring out Christmas gifts and planning holiday baking adventures. This year I decided we should start the two-and-a-half-month glide into the hap-hap-happiest time of the year with a family pumpkin carving event. Mark groaned a bit.

I argued back by telling him that even after sending everyone in our CSA home with a jack-o'-lantern-sized pumpkin and giving away several others besides, we had more pumpkins than even *I* wanted decking out the front porch. I calculated that we had just enough for each of our children's families. The cost of receiving one: coming over for a simple soup supper and being willing to carve up a pumpkin. So we held our First Annual Pumpkin Carving Extravaganza last week.

Mark was pretty sure our children accepted the invitation to be polite, so I double-checked. But it's not as if any of my sons-in-laws would say, "Well to be honest, Lisa, the idea sucks." As it was, Sarah and Jason had planned to go away to San Francisco for the weekend. What Mark saw as an opportunity to cancel I perceived as a minor obstacle.

I shooed him away and spent the afternoon making jack-o'-lantern sugar cookies like I used to make for the girls' Halloween parties in their elementary school days. I made butternut squash bars, autumn stew, homemade bread chock-full of seeds and nuts, and apple cider served in carved out apples. The carved-out apple idea came from Megan Anna which was clear proof, I told Mark, that our daughters were *not* just being polite. I think he groaned again.

But eat and carve away we did. And my dear son-in-law Aubry said, as he was helping clean the kitchen after our soup and multi-grain bread, "I love creating traditions around holidays. I especially like celebrating fall ones. Thanks for organizing this. We should do it again next year." Needless to say, I voted his jack-o'-lantern the best of the bunch.

Partly Mark doesn't much like the holidays because he's basically a rut person and holidays interrupt the rut. I'm trying to get him to see that October 15 to January 2 could be one glorious and long holiday rut if he chose to see it that way. He's actually come a long way, moving from one who barely tolerated Christmas to finding it meaningful enough to actually *move* him. It was a theological change for him, one that he'll undoubtedly write about later.

I'll defend traditions still (though not the commercializing of holidays, which is Mark's primary and very valid complaint), because rituals help us pause and take note of what has changed since we stood side by side in this place, or side by side with other family members or a different community a year ago, or 10, 15, or 35 years ago. Rituals connect us to our clan, to friends who become family when our clan is far away, and to our various cultural heritages that remind us of our histories.

So I'll remember with fondness trick-or-treating with our daughters as the first flurries of snow fell in Illinois, even though I dismayed that snow would fall so soon with all the neighborhood children wearing skimpy costumes made of nothing that kept the cold from chilling their bones. We mothers and fathers commiserated on this most ridiculous ritual, yet knew we would be back next year, hoping the flurries held off until November.

I remember years of Christmas Eve services and singing "Silent Night" in the dark as we passed the fire of our *dripless* candles (that dripped anyway) down the rows, brother to sister, husband to wife, neighbor to neighbor until the whole sanctuary glowed with soft, holy light. Only a community remembering together the birth of Jesus could create that magic.

Silty Clay Rites

Today the local clan of pot throwers inducted me into the tribe. The most recently added member had the honor of reciting the words of initiation and placing two smears of silty clay on my cheeks, after which the class filled the building with *ie-ie-ie-ee* war cries and various other hoots and hollers.

I pulled up my first six-inch cylinder on the potter's wheel, the accomplishment that earned me the right of membership. Not an easy task, that. Took multiple tries to get it right and I'm still working at getting it right consistently.

Tuesday and Thursday mornings this winter I'm sitting in on the beginning ceramics class at George Fox University. My friend and colleague, professor Mark Terry, teaches the course and I'm learning about more than ceramics as I observe him work the craft of teaching and community-building around the art of throwing, sculpting, coiling, and pinching clay.

In hard years keeping traditions offers space to imagine how life might be different next year, one more year removed from the particular pain of the one in which we stand. Observing traditions also reminds me that God does not change and has stood always, loving and sustaining all of creation since the beginning. God holds us in our pain and delights in our joy and will do so forever. That gives me hope.

I admit to sharing some of Mark's preference to see holidays pass as just another day. Much of what he distains is how holidays have been co-opted by commercial interests so that opportunities to embrace family and community traditions around the holidays become a scheduling nightmare, a financial drain, and a disappointment. Perhaps that's why I'm drawn most to simple celebrations, like candlelight services at Christmas and pumpkin carving events.

As we cleaned up after the First Annual Pumpkin Carving Extravaganza, Mark agreed we'd had a nice evening and that this might well become a pleasant family tradition. Maybe now that our family has multiplied into four families, pumpkin carving will become our way to gather together to usher in the holiday season, to take note year after year of what has changed between and among us, and to name what we can count on to stay the same.

I wore my clay stripes back to my department. Cliff thought I was treating a rash with some sort of cucumber mud mask. I suppose mostly we only expect the young to engage in rituals that include public initiations, assuming those on the up side of 50 have no rites or rituals left, except the ones that come at the end of life, like retirement and dying.

Historically, rites of passage moved people from one significant role to another—from childhood to maidenhood, maidenhood to motherhood, boyhood to manhood. The transitional time was seen as potentially dangerous, a tenuous period where the trajectory of life could get thrown off balance and head another way. To be sure an individual transitioned successfully he or she went through skill training and education under the guidance of elders, allowing them to learn the community's history and wisdom. And when those individuals were perceived as ready, they were given a challenge to test them, to prove to themselves and the community that they had earned their new position and the rights and responsibilities that came with it.

Professor Terry shows us how to be in community with each other—how to teach, learn from, and encourage each other. So we build trust and become trustworthy, celebrate accomplishments with ritual, and earn the right to critique each other's work. We are being reminded that good art, maybe even the best art, is gestated and born in community. I am reminded of the intricate baskets woven by the Nambian women I visited in a Ugandan village. I watched them work at their art while we sat together on mats outside their homes as they wove their lives and stories into beautiful baskets.

Part of my induction ritual involved destroying that first vessel, cutting it in half with a wire which allowed me (and anyone else in the room) to examine the even or unevenness in the walls, the symmetry or lack of symmetry, the flaws and beauty. Destroying the piece reminded me that rights gained don't grant me absolute control over my destiny and skills. Cutting the cylinder in half also reminded me that things I make still aren't primarily mine, but belong in some important ways to my community, and to God. And finally, destroying that vessel reminded me that I can let go of things I want to keep—whether they are taken by force, fate, or let go by choice.

These are worthy lessons. Without a ritual I may forget them. Instead I will always remember the pride of drawing up my first six-inch cylinder, measuring it to be sure, and then releasing ownership as I cut it in two.

Now that I've been initiated, I've gained some rights and obligations as a potter. I am free to go to the wheel without invitation or permission. I can access the pottery lab and throw in the evenings, mornings, or weekends. I have also accepted an obligation to help, as best I can, classmates struggling with clay.

Today's ritual inspired me to think about finding ways to validate the acquisition of new skills and to acknowledge the humility and responsibility that comes with them. Not until recently in human history did we stop inducting practitioners and apprentices into artisan or practitioner communities where wisdom and secrets passed from generation to generation. I am grateful for the faithfulness and patience of these teachers to see that an art or skill be kept alive within a community of practitioners or artists. I wonder at how much we have lost.

Meanwhile I think of all the potential inductions I could have celebrated with some community—perhaps my mothers and/or daughters, a few colleagues, or simply with my husband: successful bread baking, baby birthing, chick and hen keeping, beekeeping, farming, classroom teaching.

Maybe Mark and I will invite some interested students to our honey harvest next August (we always have students interested in beekeeping). We'll take the first honey we run through the sieve, he'll smear some on my cheeks and I on his, and we'll all give a hoop and holler as we induct each other into the sacred order of honeybee keepers. And maybe the year after that we can induct a few students who stick around throughout the year to learn the bee tending tasks and skills required throughout the fall, winter, spring, and summer before we're rewarded as we draw out some of the bee's sweet nectar in return for services rendered.

CULTIVATING COMPASSION AND JUSTICE

Morning (Mourning) Labor

From early June through early October, Wednesdays started early during our sabbatical year. Before joining Mark, who had already begun the harvest, I'd put water in a pan to boil and then pour in steel cut oats—breakfast for our midharvest break. Over the weeks we specialized. Mark picked strawberries and I the raspberries. I cut chard and kale and dug up carrots and beets. He harvested corn and broccoli and sorted through onions. Together we picked squash, beans, tomatoes, and dug up potatoes.

After harvesting I came inside to steam milk for Mark's hot chocolate and my mocha and took them out to the picnic table on the patio where we put together the crates for our Community Supported Agriculture (CSA) subscribers. I also carried out egg cartons filled with brown, blue, and dark brown eggs from our hens, as well as whatever produce we harvested during the week and held in cold storage. While Mark washed and clipped, I bundled and arranged. Sometimes we talked; sometimes we worked in silence, listening to birds, our hens, and the occasional bray from our neighbor's donkey.

Early in the season I added lavender shortbread cookies, zucchini yeast rolls, and a jar of freezer jam. Later in the season we added a pint of honey and every week we topped off the crate with herbs, and a sunflower, zinnia, or rose for color.

We finished by noon and our subscribers were welcome to pick up their crates between 2 and 6 p.m. I visited with my dear friends Marcile and Ada when they came, along with my niece, Leya, and her two lovely little girls. And when Cara came she almost always brought Lily—her delightful six-year-old who visited the hens and checked for eggs. Henry, Lily's brother, politely asked if he could pick strawberries or raspberries to eat. I always said yes, and then we negotiated a number—a trick I learned from his father when they first came. Jack, the eldest, liked to sit by the bees and meander through the forest. They called me Farmer Lisa, which I find more endearing and just as meaningful as my other professional title (Dr. McMinn).

Some took time to wander through the Fern Creek woods, eat a picnic, sit in the gazebo or the hammock. Their love of visiting Fern Creek blessed me as does the value they placed on the food we provided them every week. I was nourished by their support of our farming efforts and the faith they had in our ability to grow food. I missed our Wednesday morning ritual when our CSA season wrapped up.

Last week a reporter from our local, small-town newspaper did a story on Fern Creek. He asked if what we get paid covers our expenses and I said, "Not this year; we put in an irrigation system and raised beds. But next year, yes, next year."

I refuse to do the math on this. We farm because it is good for our soul, the soil, Fern Creek's insects and birds, and our neighbors. The energy we have to do any work at all comes from eating healthy food grown in dirt worked without petroleum-based fertilizers, pesticides, and herbicides. Our subscribers re-learn what grows in season and what it means to be neighborly as they support our efforts.

Since we can't farm for a *living* on Fern Creek's five acres, why do we do it? Why do I ponder a possible shift in my career so I have more time for tending the forest, bees, chickens, and land?

Partly because farming allows Mark and me to create and to work together, to figure out what we'll plant, how and what we'll sell, and what we'll preserve. We've become apprentices of the land together and enjoy the challenge of learning how to keep aphids from destroying the Brussels sprouts and gophers from eating the carrots. Together we forge cooperative connections with other farmers and build relationships with our subscribers.

Most of the world's workers sell their labor to get a paycheck that allows them (hopefully) to buy what they need to live. Workers in cocoa fields, manufacturing, and slaughterhouse factories are alienated from their product. They have no control over how a job is done—how to prepare an animal for death, the color of cloth they sew, or what happens to the cocoa bean after they harvest it. They are alienated from their own potential as creative beings because no creativity is required for the work they do; in fact, creativity is usually discouraged. Most of the world's workers are alienated from co-workers with whom they compete for jobs, promotions, or simply to keep from getting laid-off. Finally, they (and we) become alienated from nature because a thousand links stand between us and the earth's natural resources—the sources of our plastic, metal, cardboard, and even our chocolate, cheese, and chicken nuggets. This long link chain has rendered Earth's contributions invisible to us.

Karl Marx wrote of all this. He was concerned that the new age of industrial capitalism would take away an important part of what it meant to be human: the capacity to create, to make choices about what we create, and to live and work in communities that supported each other's work and value the natural resources from which raw materials came. Granted, Marx's economic ideas got picked up by political figures (Stalin for one) who used them to justify terrible crimes against humanity. So mostly we are uncomfortable crediting Marx with good ideas and don't much talk about his theory of labor and alienation. But in Marx's ideal world, people would choose their work and maintain some control over what they made and how they created useful products to sell, keep, or trade for others' useful products. They would feel satisfied by good work and would strengthen community relationships in the exchanges that took place. He imagined a utopia that we've never seen realized. Maybe he was imagining heaven.

But on this side of heaven, the growth of entrepreneurs, cottage industries, small family farms, and community markets in North America is reclaiming something we lost on the road to progress. These hold promise of connecting us again to values held by those who lived before.

The final week of our CSA, families took home their giant pumpkin (Lily had tagged hers several weeks ahead of time). If they wanted them, they took corn stalks and gourds to decorate their front porches. We loaded our subscribers up with potatoes and acorn, butternut, and delicata squash. And throughout the year we continued to sell eggs and honey to those who came seeking good food grown in ways that allowed the land, hens, bees, and people all to flourish.

At the conclusion of our CSA, I mourned the end of this good morning labor. But, Mark and I have already planted next year's garlic and begun to anticipate next year's season.

Empowering a Maran

A year ago I told Lisa that we really need grandchildren because we talk too much about our chickens. We have two grandchildren now who fill our lives with joy, but it didn't help reduce the chicken talk. Chickens are fascinating creatures, evidenced by how many phrases of daily speech reference them: flying the coop, feeling chicken (afraid), pecking order, coming home to roost, being henpecked, old stomping ground, no spring chicken, brooding, acting like a chicken with its head cut off, don't count your chickens before they hatch, put all your eggs in one basket, and more.

Today as I dug an irrigation ditch, the chickens did their normal thing of surrounding me so they could look for earthworms in each fresh shovel full of earth. Fact is, the early bird—or at least the boldest one—*does* get the worm. It's not so good for the earthworms, but the hens seem thrilled. I wonder if an earthworm tastes to them like a fresh, homemade oatmeal cookie tastes to me. They feasted and feasted today as I dug my 50-foot ditch.

One Maran hen with a broken toe turned out to be the most courageous of all. (Marans are a particular variety of chickens that lay a dark brown egg.) She hung out in the ditch, inches from the shovel, while others hovered at a safe distance. I tried tossing a little dirt on her once—to encourage her to give me some room to work—but it didn't faze her. She just kept pecking away at the ground, dirt on her back. Once I picked her up with the shovel and lifted her out of the ditch. She was back in a few seconds.

My mind skipped back to a year ago when we first got this hen—then an adolescent pullet about three months old. We bought two chickens that day, though one didn't live through the year. Both were terrified little critters who had never been beyond the confines of an indoor cage.

(Coincidentally, most of the 300 million laying hens in our country live inside battery cages and have no more than 67 square inches for their entire life. Imagine an 8" x 8" piece of paper as the living space for a typical hen. Thankfully, this is likely to change in the near future.)

We tried introducing our Marans to the great spaces of Fern Creek, but they huddled inside the coop, too afraid to venture into the great outdoors. Insecure, frightened little birds they were. I'm sure it didn't help when one of them was snagged by a predator—probably a raccoon that managed to reach through the fence into the hen yard. Then we had just one solitary Maran, younger than the rest of the flock and chicken as a chicken can be. Hens really do have a pecking order, and our Maran resided at the bottom.

I suppose chickens can't really be redeemed, at least not in the way that we talked about in the Conservative Baptist church I grew up in. But something quite amazing happened to this chicken with the broken toe in the course of a year. She moved from a 24/7 life in a small chicken cage to being the boldest of the flock, even if still at the bottom of the pecking order—an explorer and adventurer undaunted by a farmer with a shovel.

In these years farming at Fern Creek I have become more and more convinced that the theologians are right about us being created to be in a harmonious relationship with nature. In his fine book, *Created in God's Image,* Anthony Hoekema describes how we are built to be in relationship with God, others, and creation. This makes sense to me intellectually, but not until I started digging irrigation ditches and observing chickens did I fully understand Hoekema's point about being connected with creation. That little chicken from a year ago didn't want to hover in a battery cage all her life. Even without cognitive awareness, she wanted to be free, to hunt for earthworms and do that ridiculous waddle that all chickens do when they run. She wanted to peck for bugs in the rain, to dust bathe on sunny days, to explore and frolic and live. Today I saw a Maran chicken behaving the way Maran chickens ought to behave, and it seemed good and right, as if I have somehow been part of empowering a chicken to be what God created her to be.

The thing about chicken stories is that they are rarely just about chickens. In the process of caring for chickens, tilling the earth, nurturing strawberries and onions and squash and all sorts of other plants, I have also been released and empowered. When I left my childhood farm as a young adult, I never anticipated coming back to till the earth, but this desire to be in relationship with the land is stronger than I imagined. Hoekema is right, I think, that I was made to be connected with nature, to observe how chickens waddle and wonder what it must be like for an earthworm to be gobbled up whole, to get wet when it rains and perspire when it doesn't, to delight when a seed germinates and a plant begins journeying toward maturity. I see the same fascination with nature in Lisa who delights in the outdoors even more than I.

I guess it's called *the great outdoors* for a reason. What if God's redemptive presence in this world goes far beyond the way we understood it in my childhood church? Maybe redemption calls us to abundant living here and now—to the fullness of creation, to frolic and play and work amidst the beauty of the earth. I think we may have focused too much on the broken toes (and souls) back then, and not enough on learning to waddle.

Tending Dirt

Yesterday we took a day off from our spring farming tasks. We drove into Portland where Mark worked with our son-in-law Jason on electrical jobs in their basement and I planted starts with Sarah in her vegetable garden. They purchased the house last year and are making it into a wonderful home, which currently includes adding a bedroom, bathroom, family room, laundry room, and pantry in the unfinished basement space.

Sarah and Jason spent a chunk of time late last spring pulling debris out of the garden spot, hoping to get vegetables growing even though they were not yet living in their home. I worked with her one day last year tackling the blackberries that had claimed the spot. We all tossed berry vines, tires, boards, cans, plastic bottles, and a broken lawn chair onto a pile to be hauled away to the dump. We found a few garden treasures among the refuse: a wire sculpture of a butterfly, wind chimes, another sculpture of a fish, a glass globe. These Sarah saved, hung on the fence or gate, or placed in the rockery. Underneath all that we saw that someone had built several raised beds for growing food.

The soil in those beds simmered with life. We saw earthworms, ground beetles, centipedes, and Devil's coach horses (scary looking earwig-like bugs, but actually beneficial). The dark, loamy dirt looked ready for seeding, and seed we did. But little grew that year. Weeds prevailed, along with cabbage caterpillars, aphids, grubs, and slugs that feasted on fledging plants trying to make a go of it.

Over the winter Jason and Sarah removed the raised bed lumber, layered the garden spot with weeds, grass clippings, vegetable scraps from the kitchen, more blackberry vines, and cardboard. Then they let it sit, cooking at the slow burn of a compost pile all winter long. This spring when they pulled off the soggy, partially decomposed cardboard, then hoed and raked through the dirt, a healthy happy plot of soil whispered, "Whew! Thank you! Try again." So try they did. Sarah created rows, inserting scraps of lumber from the basement project to create stepping paths every three rows. She planted a square of carrots, a few rows of greens, and beets, and together we put in a flat of starts a farming friend brought them: red and green cabbages, broccoli, kale, and onions.

Now that they have settled in, they will be able to keep the garden weeded and watered. But even so, the patient waiting over the winter allowed the sheet composting strategy to kill weeds and make the place less hospitable to unwanted plants yet hospitable to beneficial microbes and insects. Sarah and Jason will need to stay on top of blackberries especially, pulling roots that will fight to tunnel in underground from across the fence to take back what they once conquered.

Three thoughts came to me as I reflected on this piece of garden soil reclaimed from blackberries that had been allowed to grow as cover to the garbage dumped there. One is how much dirt longs to grow things. Even when we abuse it, beat it down, poison it, and dump on it, if we clear the debris and give it time to rest—time for worms and centipedes to accomplish their miracles—the soil heals. Dirt becomes again life-nourishing soil that feeds humans, insects, birds, and a host of other creatures.

The second is that a garden left alone will become wildness. Maybe in Eden that worked out okay, but in a world where gardens groan for redemption right along with people, tending dirt is an act of grace. The strongest competitors win in wildness, which tend to be non-native species introduced at some point in the past. Non-native plants thrive because they've landed in places where their own natural competitors don't exist. Himalayan blackberries, Canada thistle, dock, and Scotch broom are some non-native plants in Oregon.

And third, farming and gardening is good for the soul. It reminds us of our humble beginnings—that we depend on food that comes from dirt to sustain our lives, and that we are part of creation and not set apart from it. It reminds us we bear the image of God.

A very good day for me generally involves a fair bit of time tending the garden. Maybe I weed flowerbeds or continue the ongoing task of pulling blackberries out of the forest by the creek. Sometimes it includes cleaning out the hen house or working on a building project with Mark. The time working alone is comfortable, as is time working with Mark or Sarah where conversation flows easily, or not at all.

I've stopped calling my teaching job my *real* job, and now refer to it as my *other* job. I'm growing more convinced that my real job—my real calling—is tending dirt.

Hoeing

I spend hours hoeing. Weeds are tenacious things, and so am I. The gardens for our CSA are too large to hoe quickly and too small to warrant the title "field" so as to justify a John Deere for weed control. So my morning routine through much of the late spring and summer involves rising early, finding my nitrile gloves, wide-brim hat, and well-used hoe, and heading to the gardens for an hour or two (or three or four) of hoeing.

Hoeing is one of the simple pleasures of life, replete with agricultural and theological meaning. Still, this week I noticed myself pondering alternatives. I began thinking that I could use my time more efficiently. Perhaps I could write another book this summer, or do more consulting, or teach an additional class, and then simply hire someone else to do all this tedious work in the gardens. Once I hire a manual laborer, maybe I could watch more baseball on television or keep up with NBA playoffs.

I stopped short when I realized what I was saying to myself. Inside my own brain I was replaying the post-World-War-II cultural shift that changed agricultural life, spiritual awareness, and daily health. People traded their small family farms for "real jobs," often selling to large agribusinesses that had their own forces of manual laborers and large equipment to keep the silos full. Before we knew what was happening, our food system conformed itself to the prevailing philosophical impetus of McDonald's—fast, efficient, productive, cheap.

I don't blame farmers for this. They often sold land farmed for decades by their ancestors, not because they wanted to watch more basketball or find office jobs, but because the economic forces of the time gave them few options. They sold for survival. Thousands of small family farms gave way to a huge food industry that fills the shelves of our grocery stores with a million permutations of processed corn, wheat, and soybeans. We struggle with high glycemic loads and low-density lipoproteins cluttering our arteries, but at least our food is cheap and abundant.

There was a time when millions of U.S. families were directly involved in food production for their own needs and those of their communities. (The 6.8 million U.S. farms in 1935 dwindled to 2.1 million by the turn of the twenty-first century, even as the population grew from 127 million to almost 300 million.) They raised chickens in the backyard, grew vegetables, and tended berries in the garden. Amidst the massive cultural shifts in agriculture, we were told to take it easy, to find office jobs and get more schooling, to always shop for the best price, to watch television, to relax, to buy more of the beer and chips whose advertisements fill our airwaves. It was going to be the good life.

Jesus said the love of money is the root of all evil. I tend to interpret this individually, as if my personal love of money will bring evil in my life. True enough. But Jesus may have had something much bigger in mind, too. Maybe collectives—families, communities, nations—can love money so much that their practices become rooted in evil. Could it be that we have loved cheap food so much we have unintentionally created economic forces that pried people away from land that had been part of their family for generations? And in the process we contributed to animal misery and corporate greed. We began thinking that food comes from the grocery store rather than springing forth from the ground and supplied with energy by the sun's radiance. Our food is cheap. We now spend ten percent of our income on food—about half of what we spent 50 years ago. But at what cost to our souls?

I feel inspired by today's back-to-the-farm movement. We see farmers' markets popping up everywhere along with community supported agriculture and backyard chickens. It's not too late to turn this around and reconnect with food and the land that produces it as our source of life.

In the quiet hours of a summer morning at Fern Creek, I hear the birds sing, watch the dew on strawberry leaves give way to another day's photosynthesis. As I chop weeds from the soil, I am reminded how easily competing forces choke out the simple goodness of life. Then again, I see the tenacity of the plants we nurture, being reminded anew of how much all creation yearns to grow. I have wide-open morning hours to ponder life and reflect on its many blessings. The morning stillness calms my soul and reminds me of the simple goodness of God's grace.

Lisa

Sex at Fern Creek

On my way from the upper garden to the lower garden I stopped to watch beetles having sex in the rocks lining the driveway. Beetle sex is not pretty, but then human sex is not particularly pretty either. Beautiful maybe, but not pretty.

I don't know how the female beetle actually *experiences* sex, but I hope less traumatically than it looks. The male and female beetles are attached end to end because he has penetrated her with a barbed penis. (I looked this up later. Magnified pictures of the male beetle penis look like gladiator weapons.) She, being the smaller of the two, is dragged behind him, walking backwards trying to keep up, traversing rapidly over and under rocks until, I suppose, he releases her, which didn't happened in my ten minutes of astute observation. Instead I witnessed three other pairings on the rocks, none of whom came unattached. I wished the males would just hold still, do their deed, and be done.

Females in the bee kingdom get even, though I doubt that's much consolation to female beetles. Fern Creek hives, like all hives, are made up mostly of female worker bees who never mate. Drones make up less than five percent of the hive, and the lucky ones (or unlucky depending on your perspective) will get to mate once with a queen from some other hive. Every hive has one queen, and she makes one nuptial flight to the stud pie in the sky and copulates with as many males as it takes to fill up her tank with the sperm that will allow her to lay hundreds of thousands of eggs in her two- to three-year lifespan. Males from all over the countryside follow the pheromone smell of these virgin queens and if they are chosen they die and fall from the sky as soon as they copulate. I wonder if they know this. Being a drone is cushy enough life in the summer, but since they do *nothing* to help the hive survive, drones get expelled by the worker bees come winter. I have seen their carcasses littering the porches of our hives in early winter.

All this makes me thankful for human sex, which has far more potential to be consensual, enjoyable, and sustainable for both men and women. We aren't the only species that values mating for life. A few others do too, like eagles, wolves and, imagine this, prairie voles. I wonder what sex looks like for them as they age, particularly after the female stops being fertile. Do they stop copulating? Or do they still copulate as a way to express their connection, to remind them that they belong to each other?

Students in my sexuality classes express curiosity about *normal* human sexual behavior. Some experts who attempt to answer that question look to the animal kingdom for answers, assuming animals have not been influenced by ads, changing cultural norms, and pharmaceutical companies trying to define "normal" to sell drugs that help everyone achieve normalcy. But the animal kingdom doesn't help overly much, given that it is full of variety which appears to be functional for each species. All life requires functional sex to propagate—even corn, apples, and green beans—but for some species, humans in particular, sex is about more than producing offspring.

Humans have sex even when they *aren't* trying to propagate, and human females (unlike most animals) continue to have sex long after fertility has ceased. We can also use sex to intentionally hurt each other or to express deep love. Human cultures attach great significance to sex and clothe it with norms and laws reflecting deeply held beliefs and values about how sex should and should not be conducted.

I want answers about normal human sexual behavior to come from grappling with God's intention for human sexuality. That sex can be pleasurable for females (capable of orgasms unlike most other animals) may suggest that God intended sex also to be for our delight and emotional connection. We learn something of giving and receiving, first to our lover and then, if children are born, to our offspring whose needs demand attention and sacrifice. Perhaps because children take such a *long* time to become independent, sex during unfertile times (and once fertility has ceased) helps keep marital bonds strong and satisfying. If we let it, a lifetime of sex can also remind us of our deep relational yearnings, knowing that these yearnings emerge from being created in the image of a God who loves and pursues us.

So what's normal sexual behavior for humans? Maybe it's sex that creates and sustains human bonds that will nurture couples, families, and communities through life. If that's the case, then we should resist letting a market economy define what normal *ought* to look like. Pharmaceutical companies make big bucks convincing men and women that they know what "normal" sex drive should look like, and in general their advertising convinces us only the beautiful get love (and sex) and that their product can fix our unacceptable features.

I am grateful for the deep emotional connection that can accompany human sexuality. Interesting as it is, beetle and bee sex does not reflect the depth and richness of healthy human sexuality. I rather like imagining a wolf pair, mated for life, who feel deep loss and grief when one precedes the other in death. Maybe, like wolves, our grief is borne from a lifetime of wandering hills together, nestling into dens, caring for our young, and drawing comfort from each other, wrapping it all in the endless grace of God.

Mark

Economics

One mid-August morning Lisa and I hopped out of bed to a day we had been anticipating for months. I suppose we didn't really hop out of bed like we did when in our 30s, but we hobbled out of bed with extraordinary eagerness for the day ahead. This was to be our first annual honey harvest day.

Italian honeybees start setting aside honey for the winter almost as soon as the previous winter winds down. April showers bring May flowers, making May a busy month for honeybees. By mid-May, the bees have stocked the pantry in the two hive body boxes, so beekeepers put some empty, smaller boxes called *supers* on top of the two hive bodies. The bees keep stashing honey in the supers, not knowing their annual rent will be collected when mid-August rolls around— payment for free housing on Fern Creek. When harvesting, we leave each colony with 70-100 pounds of honey in their hive bodies which is plenty of food for the winter.

Such was the task for our day—undoubtedly a more exciting prospect for us than for our honeybees. Still, they cooperated well enough, or at least our beekeeper suits let us think so as they protected us from potential stings. We removed supers from our four hives and situated ourselves in the potting shed, which doubles as our honey harvesting room, for a day of extracting and bottling.

Each super holds ten wooden frames which slide into our hand-cranked extractor. It takes quite a lot of spinning to get the honey out, but the soreness that settles into one's arms and shoulders is softened by the steady flow of golden honey that pours from the extractor through a double mesh filter into a 5-gallon bucket. When the bucket is about half full, we lift it onto the counter, open the honey gate, and fill jar after jar. This year we filled 56 quarts.

The day was as rewarding as we had anticipated, and quite a bit longer. Somehow I had imagined honey harvesting taking a few hours, but it took from dawn to dusk, and beyond. Getting the final honey to filter through the beeswax takes a few more days, the empty supers go back on the hives for a couple of days for the bees to clean before we pack and store them for winter.

At some point near the end of that very-long-and-very-rewarding day, I did some mental math. I imagined what 56 quarts of honey might be worth. Then I computed our equipment purchases and amortized them over ten years, and then made a rough calculation of how many hours each year we devote to beekeeping. After dividing the net value of our honey by our hours per year, I came to the humbling conclusion that Lisa and I make about two dollars per hour as beekeepers. This assumes we sell all the honey, when in reality we'll eat and give away a fair share of it.

Late that evening as we rested in our two-person hammock, I told Lisa about the economics of our beekeeping. She smiled that warm familiar smile, as I knew she would. We both chuckled. Then we started dreaming and planning for next year's beekeeping.

Why would we do such a thing when it makes no economic sense? It's the wrong question. The better question is how did we get in such a place where so many decisions in life are governed by economics? Granted, we all need to make a living—to have shelter and food—but it seems so much of daily life has become a calculus problem where we try to maximize profitability while minimizing our investment of time. So many are left alienated from their work, seeing it only as a means to an end rather than something with intrinsic goodness and reward.

Doing something for two dollars per hour makes no economic sense. And why would I even do the mental math on this if not because I have been socialized to think that my time should always be profitable?

I liked Lisa's chuckle in the hammock. It reminded me that we are both striving to avoid living by economic calculations and, instead, trying to accept the taste of honey on our biscuits and the satisfaction of good work as reward enough.

Tender Fire

Mostly I see ice crystals and opportunity where others see snow-related traffic nightmares, and when the electricity goes out, I see adventure instead of inconvenience. My cheery disposition is not always easy to live with, especially when I expect those less cheery to buck up and embrace ice crystals.

But sometimes I get a glimpse of how other people—those who feel the world holds more despair than hope—experience life. Such was a recent week where my sorrowful spirit descended into the early November darkness. A couple of significant sadnesses had broken upon our home—primarily the death of Bob, my father-in-law (Mark's stepdad) with whom Mark and I lived for a year while we built our home at Fern Creek. We all became family that year, and friends, and we cherish the year we lived with Mom and Bob as a rare gift afforded to adult children and their parents. Bob died too young for the life left in him, and his rather quick passing gave us little time to get used to the idea of living without him.

The other sadness came from a conversation with people I care about deeply. I learned of their lost faith, their mere fledgling hope that perhaps God exists.

How could any soul not be dimmed in such times?

I sat with my sadness, letting grief be okay—a right and proper response to a world that hurts. On that Tuesday, after several nights of quiet sadness, I played Solitaire (again) on the couch. My outward expression of sadness is subtle, and generally only Mark can tell when I'm seeing the groaning of the world rather than its glory.

Mark sat nearby and I know he felt both sadnesses as much as I did, but he was—at least at that moment—less affected. Maybe staying with Mom a couple nights prior to Bob's death and witnessing his death made the effect more profound to me, and maybe Mark hearing of the conversation about lost faith second hand eased some of its hardness. Or maybe Mark was simply distracting himself, caught up in what we call "the computer programming vortex" from which it is nearly impossible to call him back until he has completed whatever sub routine he's working on.

But my sadness reached through the vortex. Maybe I sighed or said something. Or maybe he just knew in the ways that husbands and wives sometimes come to know after years of marriage. He looked up, pulled himself from the vortex, and asked if I could imagine anything that would tend to my soul on this evening.

I sighed and said, "Well, I keep thinking that on any one of these fall nights I ought to go build myself a fire in the gazebo and sit with it." Not wanting to obligate him, I added, "I wouldn't need you to do it with me."

But Mark knew that I wouldn't, on that night anyway, go start a fire alone. He understands from personal and professional experience that darkness can feel too heavy to move one from Solitaire to a fire pit. He closed up his computer (and I *know* the sacrifice that required) and said, "Let's go do it. I'll change my shoes and get the flashlight."

Tears stung my eyes immediately, and I stood up and said, "I'll get newspaper and matches."

So we stumbled down to the gazebo guided by the weak beam of a flashlight whose light was mostly spent; built a teepee with newspaper, kindling, and wood; and lit us a fire. We sat side by side, listening to the creek speak to the woods as it always does in November, and the conversing of a good fire as it crackled like fires have since the beginning of time. Sometimes we talked ("Would you say fire is alive?" he asked at one point), but mostly we sat and watched and listened to the world carry on as it always does—in good times and bad, in sorrowful times and joyful, a consistent and faithful representation of God's constant presence and attention.

Meanwhile Mark's tender love wrapped me up and lifted my soul.

CULTIVATING GRATITUDE AND GENEROSITY

Lisa

Play It Again

I went into the office to pick up mail this week and one of my colleagues said, "You have a sticker on your back." She pulled it off. It was a sticker of a cat—one of six that came with Pollifax's worming medicine.

I laughed and said, "Mark and I have been passing those back and forth for the last month, putting them in unexpected places, like dashboards, toothbrushes, pillows."

"Well, he certainly got you," Claudia said.

Mark and I have taught each other how to play over the years. I loved his crazy jokes, wordplay, and the way he threw spit wads at me in ninth grade as a sign of his love. He loved my confidence in setting a target and challenging him to see which one of us could hit it with our watermelon rind. We arm wrestled (I always lost), thumb wrestled (always lost again), and played table football at restaurants with the little paper bands wrapped around our napkins folded into triangles (it took me years to learn how to flick a field goal). And he tolerates me catching him unawares as we head for bed. I turn out the last of the lights when he is nowhere near a light switch, throwing us into blackness, and then sneak up on him. He is not allowed to do this to me and I love that he honors that.

One of our most memorable playful episodes involved a PG-rated video that we made of ourselves on our tenth anniversary using our 1980s camcorder. We had stayed at the Marriott, and while I'm a bit ashamed of it now, we were merciless in our video. While staying in our wonderful room we noted that we could buy wine or porn flicks—both discouraged by the Mormon Church to which J.W. Marriott belongs. So we wrote and videotaped a rap and had a ridiculous amount of fun doing so. We looked utterly foolish, but since I can step to a rhythm slightly better than Mark can, I looked slightly less foolish than he did.

Sometime later when a group of friends were over, I thought we should share the video. Mark did not. I went to get it, he stole it from me, and we literally chased each other through the house, out a window on the second floor, and onto the roof. (Yes, we had children at this point—three impressionable daughters, who have since found their own rooftop adventures.)

Mark threatened to destroy the tape unless I promised to stop trying to show it to people. I sighed mightily in defeat, believing that he would indeed rip the tape from its casing if I did not acquiesce; and to this day I think only our children have laid eyes on our rap rendition called, "The Marriott."

It's been many years since we've chased each other on rooftops, but we'll still race to the finish when we're biking and leave stickers for each other to find in unsuspecting places. I wore one on my back for an afternoon last week, thinking Mark had just been giving me a tender pat on the back. Come to think of it, the sticker *was* a love pat.

Sometimes Mark and I have to remember to play. We have sometimes gone months at a time without playing, years even.

Yesterday morning while Mark stood in the shower washing his hair, I felt that popping warmth toward him that can still overwhelm me. This delight surprises me after so many years of comfortable living side by side. I told him I loved him before I left the bathroom. "Hmmm, I love you too," he muffled through the shampoo, "though that was rather random."

I walked over to the shower, pulled the curtain aside a bit and said, "It was either that or dousing you with a pitcher of cold water."

"Hmm..." he said again. "I appreciate your choice."

I love that man. My partner, soul mate, playmate.

Mark

Choosing Gratitude

Last week Lisa and I were plagued with a sour spirit toward one another that lasted several days. Life went on, and we were civil enough to each other, but both of us wrestled with our internal angst. It started with a conversation about how best to help someone we know who has substantial need, which triggered memories of long-standing differences that are mostly irresolvable, and then settled into a few days of private struggle for both of us.

I suppose every married person could find one thing or another to change about her or his partner. Okay, maybe even two or three things. There is a thing or two I would change about Lisa if I could, and she has some things she would change about me. We both maintain our mental lists, which are surprisingly short considering we have had several decades to add to them. Still, it's strange how powerful these short wish lists can be when we allow ourselves to dwell on them, especially considering the many qualities we admire in one another. After a few days, we settled back into our normal routine of seeing the good in one another and counting our blessings.

A few years back, two psychologist friends published a fascinating research study on gratitude. They asked college students to journal at the end of the day, with half of them instructed to write about daily hassles and half to write about their gratitude. At the end of the journaling period, those in the gratitude group showed all sorts of benefits when compared with those in the hassles group: they exercised more, had fewer physical complaints, were more optimistic, felt better about life, and were more likely to help others.

And so it is with marriage. We can spend our internal energy looking at the messiness of living with the other, or we can invest our thoughts in grateful reflection toward the other. It's our choice—a choice with consequences for how we experience life, and life together.

Yes, this is a bit oversimplified. There are those who are in truly terrible situations involving abuse and recurrent infidelity and criminality. I'm not arguing for a naïve view of every marriage, but most of us married folks are in relationships that are generally functional and include ample opportunity for gratitude. Most of us face a daily choice whether we will maintain our mental journals as records of daily hassles or grateful recollections of another day lived with our life partner.

Shortly after emerging from my three days of angst with Lisa, the fourth Thursday of November rolled around, reminding the country of our need to give thanks. We gathered with 15 people at Fern Creek, sharing all sorts of food, good conversation, laughter, and even a game of Taboo. We enjoyed our last Brussels sprouts and carrots from the garden, potatoes stored from the August harvest, cauliflower from the local grocery store (because ours stopped producing a few weeks prior), a lentil loaf brought by our vegan daughter, pumpkin and apple pies brought by another daughter, and mushroom gravy from yet another. Lisa made an amazing dressing, and we had the perfunctory Thanksgiving olives and cranberry sauce. The meat-eating half of our group enjoyed the free-range turkey.

Thanksgiving food is amazing enough, but I think the greater part of the tradition is simply the reminder of the choice we face. Will we ponder our troubles or reflect gratefully on the blessings of life? Once a year we set a day aside to remember how we hope to live every other day.

As the designated grace-giver for Thanksgiving meals, I decided to be avant-garde this year and ask people to keep their eyes open for our prayer together. I crafted my Thanksgiving prayer in advance during the morning hours, between peeling potatoes and slicing carrots alongside my life partner, which is an especially appropriate time for gratitude:

> Dear God,
>
> We offer this Thanksgiving prayer with our eyes open, attentive to the world for which we give thanks:
>
>> For new life, and old life, and life in the middle.
>> And for the passage from one season to the next,
>> blessed by the grace of your presence and provision.
>>
>> For those who have gone before us, teaching us
>> how to mash potatoes, bake bread, carve turkeys,
>> and grow carrots from the earth.

For the marriages and adoptions and child-bearing
and child-rearing that brings us together as family
in one place today.

For the abundance of this earth, and for all the
life that springs from it. For the creative diversity of
the food we enjoy—cauliflower, lentils, cranberries,
olives, grains, and beans, and so much more.

And thank you for the turkey.

We offer you our thanks for this abundance
of life and ask that you continually teach us how
to spread your blessings throughout the earth,
offering peace and hope and food to those in need.

I offer these words of thanks in the name of Jesus,
the Eternal Word who came and lived among us,
showing how much you love this world,
and how much you love us.

Amen

Saying grace before meals seems to be a dying tradition in our time, but I hope we never lose the discipline of saying grace in our lives—living with eyes open to the beautiful blessings all around us.

Lisa

Becoming an Old Woman (in the West)

I turned 53 this summer. To anyone over, say, 63, that will sound young enough. To those younger than about 43, I will seem old-ish, and I'll be so old to those under 20 that the nice ones will treat me with gentle kindness for fear that I might break and the rest will see me as irrelevant and/or invisible.

This may not be true, but it reflects one of my fears.

The year I turned 40 a student told me she looked forward to 40 and streaks of gray in her hair because people would take her more seriously and the angst of being young would feel less angsty. Wise words from a 19-year-old.

For my birthday Mark took me to an adventure park in the forest near Haag Lake where one gets harnessed in and then climbs into trees and then sways, crawls, swings, and zips from tree to tree through an ever increasingly challeng-

DIRT AND THE GOOD LIFE

ing and higher-off-the-ground ropes course. It felt good to know I had the upper body strength to accomplish each task, however aware we were that most folks—well, all others actually—were a good bit younger than us.

On my birthday card Mark wrote: *I love how this year has demonstrated again your lifelong love for learning. Your pottery is amazing* [note: not yet, but I hold out hope], *your desire for a cow amusing, and your tattoo—well, never mind.*

So there, it's out there. I may want a cow to milk someday, which Mark isn't sure about, and I'm getting a tattoo in two weeks, which Mark sort of hates. I've wanted one for about 20 years now, so it is not an impulsive grasp at youth. The tattoo will be over my right shoulder blade, a botanical drawing of a fern—three fronds, one still unfurling. Ferns have been a significant symbol to me for nearly as long as I've wanted a tattoo. I resonate with the way a fern, in order to grow, must unfurl and open itself to whatever comes. Whatever comes will include sun, rain, hot, and cold, but also the possibility of being nibbled or broken. The fern reminds me that I need to do the same. I need to release my hold on myself, open my hands to whatever God permits to come my way and embrace its impact on me as part of who I am to become.

Growing old requires a fair bit of that, especially as a woman living in the Western Hemisphere. In addition to feeling as though people took me more seriously, once I turned 40 I felt I could graciously back out of the competition to be beautiful in a young sort of way. I still obsessed about my weight and my clothes adequately enough to consider myself a good Western woman, but some of the angst surrounding that eased.

But 53 even feels old-ish to me. So I need to stay open to the broken fronds that increasingly become part of "maturing." And most of all, I need to accept changing roles rather than fight them. So yes, some of my students will see me as so old they can't imagine I have anything to teach them, but a lot of them are willing to hold off judgment a week or two to see if I can hold their attention. And increasingly students and other idealistic young souls wanting to learn how to live a life more connected to God's earth volunteer to come dig in the dirt with us. They think we have something to teach them, and maybe we do.

So I'm grateful for life—every day of it. Some days have been painful, most rather ordinary, and a good many wonderfully extraordinary. What a gift to have made it to 53! I think of friends who have not—Bill who drowned the summer after we graduated from high school, Margaret Rose who died too young of cancer at 42—so many I could name.

My friend Marcile, who is about 20 years my senior, said her 50s were a great decade. So far I have experienced them similarly. So much goodness! This has been the decade for adding chickens and farming to my life, and granddaughters and shifting roles in my children's lives, my mothers' lives. May God give me the grace to accept whatever God allows—the gift of each sun-filled day and the pain of each bruised frond—all of it shaping me still.

Mark

His and Hers Vacation (His)

As college professors, Lisa and I have our fall months booked with teaching, grading, meetings, writing, grading, advising, mentoring, and grading. Okay, so grading isn't my favorite thing to do, but I like everything else. These full fall schedules have prevented us from seeing the New England autumn leaves, until this year when our sabbatical allowed us to venture eastward. We had a great time hiking, talking, looking at beautiful scenery, and eating amazing food. This was our first vacation together in several years, other than "writing vacations" when we took our laptops to fun places and wrote half of each vacation day. We planned no writing on this trip, but rain changed our plans and we found ourselves at the Bangor Mall Starbucks writing essays on His and Hers Vacation.

Vacations make you think big thoughts, especially vacations that involve breathtaking views and exhilarating hikes.

But vacations also come with stressors, like the GPS. As I wrote and looked across the table at Lisa, I guessed she might, at the very same moment, also be writing about our GPS, but with a very different perspective. Almost every moment of every day in New England was delightful, except for a few directional challenges in our rented Chevrolet Aveo.

I was the designated driver on the trip because Lisa loves looking outside at the beautiful scenery as we drive. I like looking, too, but am anxious enough to keep my eyes on the road. Lisa has almost no anxiety about anything, including which lane she drives in when scenery is beautiful, so I drive while she is freely enamored with the beauty of God's creation. I love this about Lisa. She helps me appreciate natural beauty. But I also like driving when we're in beautiful places because this way we can both live to enjoy God's lovely creation for years to come. Being the designated driver comes with the responsibility of figuring out which way to turn when we encounter a "T" in the road.

Several years ago Lisa got me a GPS for my birthday. Like us, our GPS is aging; and also like us, our GPS cannot be updated with any extant computer operating system. Still, I like technology and trust this old GPS quite a lot. Lisa doesn't like technology and much prefers to rely on the occasional roadside sign or a map. When I'm looking at or listening to the GPS, Lisa routinely reminds me that she would just look at the map if it were up to her. But on this trip we didn't actually have a map, which meant we had a choice between the GPS or Lisa's internal intuitive map, which honestly isn't that good.

The voice on my GPS is a woman's voice, so I found myself being the only male in the car torn between two women's opinions. It's tough when I trust the other woman's directions more than my own wife's, but that is often the case. We had a few tense moments on our trip, always involving the anxiety I feel about how to respond to Lisa in light of the "other woman."

Despite these fleeting tensions, our trip was amazing. We hiked up mountainsides and down again, reminding ourselves of how much life we have left in these 50-something bodies of ours. We witnessed brilliant colors in the trees that surrounded us, carried by leaves preparing to die so they can become humus for next year's new life. Our conversations were varied and rich, and wise, I think. We spoke again and again of our gratitude for life.

Sometimes it surprises me how much more there is to learn about Lisa. After all these years of living side by side, she still surprises me with her quick wit, with childhood stories I haven't heard before, and with her quick and seamless transitions back and forth between profound reflection and routine matters of daily life. Our hikes reminded me of this as our conversation leaped from the colors of beautiful leaves, to the alternative life paths we could imagine having pursued, to stories of her growing up years, to dreams for the future. I feel grateful for this life partner who helps make my life so rich and abundant.

Almost every day one of us says to the other, "Have I told you today that I love you?" The other, familiar with the phrase, responds, "No, I don't think so. I love you, too." We smile familiar smiles and relish this good life, replete with so many blessings.

Lisa

His and Her Vacation (Hers)

As we hiked down the Ladder Trail in Acadia National Park, we took turns naming alternative lives we could have imagined if we had chosen different paths earlier on.

Let me back up a minute for some context. Earlier that same day we had hiked the three-mile Jordan Pond trail—a delightful trail around a large pond (we'd call it a lake in Oregon). A good chunk of the trail was made of raised planks, a boardwalk of sorts. Delightful. We wanted another three-mile hike to round out the day, but decided to keep it easy as we had climbed our mountain in the White Mountains of New Hampshire a couple of days earlier. That challenging and rewarding hike was reminiscent of a backpacking trip I took with my good friend, Jana, two of our daughters, and Kate (another teenager living with us at the time).

So Mark and I planned to take it a bit easier in Acadia. We created a three-ish mile loop that looked charming on the map. It started on Emery Trail and after a brief flat start through gentle woodlands we came upon a short stone staircase headed up the mountain. "Cool," we thought.

We turned the corner and saw more stairs heading straight up the mountain. After about 762 steps we met two women coming down. "Cool stairs," I said.

"And a *lot* more to go," they answered.

At stair 3,487 we came across three rangers working on the path and applauded their efforts, having moved enough rock on Fern Creek to know hard work when we saw it. They grunted, I think in appreciation. Probably they expected to have to haul out two 50-plus-year-old folks who got themselves into something way beyond their stamina level. We didn't see anyone else on the trail that day. That should have been a hint.

About 987 steps later (it may have been 997, I lost count), we made it to the top. Along the way we saw valley after valley of golds, yellows, greens, and reds. As we climbed higher, the harbor, islands, and blue-upon-blue met the horizon with dots of dirt and water as land and sea stretched as far as we could see.

We don't have the pictures to prove our accomplishment because I thought we had captured all the diversity possible in our previous hiking and so neglected to bring my camera. Still, at every view point Mark suggested I return to the car, back down the 7,681 stone steps to get the camera. He said he'd be willing to sit and wait for me. As I said, we don't have the pictures to prove it.

Once at the top we assumed we'd walk along the ridge for a while before heading down. By this time we had pulled out the map and saw all the squiggly lines jam packed together that meant we'd be climbing as straight down as we had straight up. I don't know how I missed that when we were scouting out a possible hike. I, the map person, should have known better.

So instead of a level ridge that would allow our legs a brief break, we came immediately to the Ladder Trail marker, a very well-named trail actually. Going down uneven steps hewn of stone with no railing—well, I just thought of Polly, Eustace, and Puddleglum climbing the steps to the giant's palace in C.S. Lewis's *The Silver Chair* and remembered it turned out okay for them in the end, even if they did almost get eaten by those giants.

So, to distract ourselves we talked about alternative paths we might have taken in life. We learned two things. First, our dreams show how very different we are and how nicely we have moderated toward the other. For instance, one of Mark's paths included being a corporate man who wore suits to work, lived in a condo on the river in Southwest Portland, and had all the latest techno gadgets because his job demanded that he keep abreast of such things. One of my dreams included being a homesteader, living off the grid, heating our home with wood, using lanterns and candles at night, writing letters we'd send by post when we went to town once a week for supplies and to pick up the week's mail. As I said, we've moderated a lot.

The second thing we learned is that we have found creative and generous ways to incorporate aspects of one another's alternative lives into the one we each currently live. I typed these words into my iPad while sitting at a Starbucks in Bangor, Maine.

But still, I prefer using a map to get me places, and I neither trust the lady who lives in our GPS, nor do I like her annoying voice ("When possible make a legal U-turn" she tells me, which translated means "Hey, you, yes you, idiot driver, *follow my directions!*"). I prefer, if I get lost, to find my own way back.

Which highlights a difference in how Mark and I vacation. I figured, let's just drive into Bar Harbor, park, and walk around until we find a coffee shop or someplace we might want to eat. I don't much mind not having a *plan*. Mark, he likes a *plan*. I think it gives him a sense of control since vacations can be so unpredictable.

He likes predictability ("Don't you ever just long for a chain restaurant when we're on vacation?" he asked. I gave him a look of incredulity, which was the most polite way I could think of answering his question.) We drove an hour to the Starbucks in Bangor. Not that there aren't coffee shops in Southwest Harbor, but there are no Starbucks. I must admit though, that Starbucks makes a most excellent soy hot chocolate for Mark and soy mocha for me. Besides, it was a rainy day and I was still recovering from the descent down the Ladder Trail.

Oh yes, the Ladder Trail. I failed to mention the ladder part was literal. We thought we had come to a dead end in the trail only to discover we were expected to descend down the face of rocks on a metal ladder that had been somehow attached to the rock. Not for the faint-hearted, that. We had three of these ladders to descend, the final one being the most challenging, especially for the short-legged hiker. But it was exhilarating too, and actually more exhilarating than terrifying. Undoubtedly the Ladder Trail, staircase and all, will be our most memorable Acadia National Park hike.

We found our blended vacation style on this trip. To make that happen required a generosity of sorts—the willingness for both of us to let go of our individual notions of a perfect vacation so that we could craft one that reflects what we both love. Future vacations will likely include lots of hiking and Starbucks, maps and GPSs, bed and breakfasts and hotels. It's not seamless, but nearly so. And this has been a most exquisite week.

Mark

Surprised by Generosity

The big, remarkable events of the world fill our webpages and nightly news broadcasts, but sometimes the simple graces of life touch us most deeply and remind us how goodness still permeates our fallen world. Sometimes a common encounter intersects with uncommon kindness, bringing a glow of warmth and hope, making me a better soul.

This story of uncommon kindness is about shingles—not the disease involving a recurrence of the childhood chickenpox virus (which I know about because Lisa just had it)—but the asphalt gravelly things we put on our roofs to blockade Oregon rain. I've been building a potting shed with a 7:12 roof, which didn't sound that steep when I researched it on the Internet. It turns out 7:12 is no easy roof to install. Gravity wants to call me back down to earth before I can put four roofing nails in each new shingle. The first challenge, however, was simply finding the shingles—ones that match the shingles on the rest of the house.

Larry, whose last name I don't know, works for Allied Materials in Medford, Oregon. He doesn't know my last name either, or my first name for that matter; we hadn't met before my out-of-the-blue phone call yesterday morning. I imagined him scurrying about his desk where his cup of morning coffee resided, juggling the paperwork, dispatch, and customer service demands of a building supply outlet, when the phone rang. On the other end was this guy from Newberg looking for the smallest imaginable quantity of an obscure shingle—2 bundles of Landmark Premium Weathered Wood.

"Is that a Certainteed shingle?"

"Yes, I think so," I answered.

"We probably don't have it in stock, but let me look."

"Thanks for looking."

A long pause followed. Thankfully, he didn't force me to listen to "I Shot the Sheriff" or some other cheesy telephone-hold-music, but I'm so accustomed to the music that the silence daunted me some. Had my cell phone dropped the call? Or maybe Larry just decided I wasn't worth the time? I almost interrupted the silence to see if Larry was still there, but I restrained myself, waiting patiently for good news.

Eventually Larry spoke. "No, sorry, we don't have it. You probably need it today, huh?"

"Well, I bought the last three bundles from the Tigard store yesterday, and my wife and I are driving south on I-5 for a brief vacation in the redwoods. I thought I would check the other Allied stores along I-5." (Lisa piloted as I sat in the passenger seat with my list of addresses and phone numbers for the Salem, Eugene, and Medford stores. My strategy involved starting with Medford, then working my way north to the Eugene and Salem calls.)

Larry answered, "Hold on a minute. Let me check Eugene and Salem for you."

"That's great! You're doing all my work for me."

After another long pause, "No, I'm sorry. None of our stores has that in stock."

"Okay, thanks for checking. I appreciate your time."

I clicked the little red hang-up button on my Blackberry, disappointed with the results but touched by the kindness of someone who had gone out of his way to try to help me. It gave me optimism for the day, knowing there are good guys still, one of whom worked in Medford.

After scratching off Salem, Eugene, and Medford from my list, I called another building supply store in Portland. Not in their Portland store, they said, but they carried that shingle in Vancouver. So I wouldn't get the shingles today on our drive south, but somehow I would find the time to make the time-consuming round trip to Vancouver and buy shingles later. Good enough.

My vibrating phone startled me. It showed an unfamiliar number, but girded with my optimism for the day, I picked it up. "This is Mark."

"Hi Mark, this is Larry from Allied in Medford. After we talked, I called one of my competitors in Medford to see if he carried that shingle. He doesn't, but their Clackamas store does. Here is the phone number…"

After thanking him a half dozen times, I clicked the red button again, sat back in the seat, and reflected on what just happened. I was an unknown guy with a trivial, non-profitable order. He must get dozens of commonplace requests like this every day, but somehow Larry showed uncommon grace to me, going out of his way to track down shingles, even if it meant sending my business to a competitor.

Everyone's busy. Common tasks and distractions fill every day. But sometimes a common event becomes uncommon because one person is willing to give generously to another—offering a gift of time or human warmth when none might reasonably be expected. The clouds part and a ray of sun warms a spot of earth.

Most of the major world religions teach something we call the "Golden Rule" in Christianity—treat others the way you want to be treated. Practicing the Golden Rule doesn't have to involve taking a bullet for a friend or saving the world from cataclysm through heroic efforts. Most often we experience the Golden Rule in the simplest events of life, like when the bank teller at our local credit union calls me by name and asks how farming is going this year.

If I ever buy shingles again, I'm going to Allied Materials. And I'll think of Larry.

Lisa

Valentine's Day

I'm in a pottery class and find myself surprised by how delightfully consuming it is. I'm actually liking my early attempts to create useful and interesting vessels. And so far when I've brought pieces home to work on them Mark has not said: "*That's* interesting." in the same tone we used when Megan Anna came home from first grade and gave us a pinch pot she made at school.

I decided to make Mark a manly mug for Valentine's Day. It's a slab piece—big, textured, with a round bit of clay at the base of the handle that looks like a screw head holding it on. I hoped to glaze and fire it in time for Valentine's Day, but that didn't happen. I wanted to fill it with all things chocolate. A specialty packet of chocolate drinking cocoa, a bag of fair trade baking chips, a fair trade mint chocolate bar, a coupon for my chocolate pudding cake, a dark chocolate brownie mix. I realize it will spill over the mug a bit.

But since the mug wasn't ready, I gave him the chocolate in bags and envelopes throughout the day, and the mug will come soon enough—a late Valentine's Day gift.

Every year Mark and I tell each other that we are not going to observe Valentine's Day. By that we mostly mean we aren't going to buy each other gifts. The gifts seem cliché, and we like to think that we are above cliché. But celebrate we do, in spite of ourselves. Our first year at Fern Creek Mark finished installing the oven just in time for us to bake up a Papa Murphy's Take 'n' Bake pizza. We ate on a card table in the middle of what later became our family room, full of the dust and debris from the kitchen cabinet installation and the stonework for our fireplace. I scrounged up a candle, and we ate on two plates from Goodwill since all our belongings were packed away in storage until we finished the house.

The next year I created a romantic candlelight dinner for two in our bedroom, and another year hosted one in the loft upstairs. This year we had dinner back in the bedroom, though if it hadn't been raining we would have dined in the gazebo with a string of white lights and candles framing our space and the music of the creek for background.

All that said, my general response to Valentine's Day had been to mock it as another holiday created by greedy capitalists. My issue was not so much that Valentine's Day promotes a gushy week of cheap romance, but that Hallmark created it to get us to buy cards, and then Tiffany & Co. and Hershey jumped on board, and *voilà!* A day to celebrate love and romance became another month to spend money and consume stuff we don't need. But when I learned that Hallmark didn't create Valentine's Day, it became more acceptable to me to embrace the holiday, even if doing so makes me feel like a cliché sellout to consumerism.

The Roman Catholic Church recognizes three Valentines who might have been the St. Valentine behind Valentine's Day. All of them in various ways are connected to fostering love and lovers. The Church declared February 14 to be Valentine's Day around 498 AD. As is true of nearly all religiously observed days, pagan fertility rituals made their way into the mix, and sometimes it is hard to tease out which observance came first. Since birds become fertile and begin mating mid-February (our hens certainly pick up their egg laying in February!), France and England thought the day should be given over to romance. As long ago as the sixteenth century, secret and not-so-secret lovers made each other cards and gave small tokens of love on February 14 when face-to-face expressions of love felt too forward. Cards started being mass-produced in the 1840s, and now about one billion valentine cards are purchased each year. Women buy a whopping 85 percent of them. I imagine that includes all the mothers buying those punch-out valentines for their children's parties at school. (Why we encourage first graders to observe Valentine's Day is a bit of mystery to me. What sort of early socialization are we offering? An early exercise in consumerism in the name of love? Ah, I digress....)

At any rate, for the sake of a bunch of relationships between men and women I have to hope most of those valentines purchased by women are for children's parties.

But why *not* enthusiastically join a 400-year-old tradition of celebrating romance and love one day a year? I want to set the last of my hesitation aside and jump into the challenge of finding creative ways to say, "I love you, I'm thinking about you today, and I'm glad it's you and me walking this road two-by-two" without having to use Hallmark, diamonds, florists, or heart-shaped boxes of chocolate. Actually, writing that out on a piece of paper and slipping it into Mark's wallet would be pretty sweet, or writing it out ten different ways and hiding each one in various places for Mark to discover throughout the day might be meaningful, too. Maybe I'll do that next year. But why wait until next year? Maybe I'll do it next month after all the post-Valentine's Day dust settles and the chocolate hearts, valentine cards, and knickknacks go away.

Romance is good. Love better yet. Here's to gratefully joining a history of romance and love-making. Happy Valentine's Day.

Mark

Trivia

I recently read that 80 percent of a plant's mass comes from sunshine, and only 20 percent from soil. As Lisa and I were pulling out dying raspberry, tomato, cucumber, pepper, and cauliflower plants during a mid-November week, I pondered these numbers. Most of the mass cradled in our arms and stuffed in our wheelbarrow had less to do with our beautiful Oregon soil and the organic fertilizer, coffee grounds, and compost we add to it and more to do with the solar energy coming from above.

Perhaps successful marriage is similar. Maybe about 20 percent of a healthy marriage comes from the personality of each partner with the other 80 percent coming from outside energy shining through each partner. If so, it becomes important for both husband and wife to live as well and as fully as possible, to be bathed in the grace of a good life, and then to allow these experiences to illumine and warm the relationship.

Lisa is remarkably good at this. She is an optimistic soul, always looking for adventure and ways to learn. And she brings this home to me, talking about significant conversations, updating me on what she is reading, and even crafting extemporaneous trivia quizzes. I think the trivia quiz idea is her way of engaging me fully in the conversation, to get me beyond the perfunctory husbandly, "Oh, that's nice." By asking a question—even a trivial one—she is looking for a real conversation.

Last week we were doing our monthly overnight stint at the local homeless shelter for women and children. As the women were retiring for the night, Lisa and I chatted in the dining room. I could tell a trivia quiz was coming, related to current events she had discovered throughout the day as she prepped for a talk. She started by asking who the top grossing female actor is. Graciously, she gave me ten yes/no questions to help me guess the right person. I didn't. Then we moved on to the top grossing male actor. Again, I failed, but I still enjoyed the adventure she was creating for me. Then she asked what I knew about James LeBon.

"I've never heard of James LeBon," I said.

"Really? You don't know who James LeBon is?" She looked absolutely incredulous.

"No, sorry. Can you give me a hint?"

"He plays football for the Miami Heat."

At this point I lost composure and probably even some civility and laughed about as hard as I have in the past decade. And Lisa, being a good sport, began laughing almost as hard when I explained that *LeBron* (first name, with an r)

James (last name) plays *basketball* (an indoor sport, not involving pigskin) for the Miami Heat. I'm sure the women in the shelter wondered what had happened to their hosts. We laughed a long time, and several times again over the next week.

When Lisa offers her silly quizzes, and when we laugh about the outcomes, we open the window for solar energy to flood in. She brings the fresh experiences of her day (however trivial they are) into our relationship where we can enjoy them together. I love that she cares to enter the world of her sports-fan husband, knowing it stretches her beyond her vocabulary and knowledge—and far, far beyond her natural interests.

The example I have just given is trivia, but the same pattern holds for more important matters. This week I have been updating an old text that I authored in 1996, writing about how much differently I view psychology because I am married to a sociologist. Lisa brings her professional ideas to our dinner table, helping me think differently—and better, I think—than my psychological training alone would allow. And I've heard her admit to the converse, too, that my daily experiences in psychology help her think differently about her work in sociology. Our rich conversations challenge and stretch us.

I love spending hours of every week with Lisa, even after all these years of marriage. But I also love that we have learned to give each other open space to learn and experience life apart from each other, and then to bring the mysteries and surprises of life back to our marriage. These open spaces warm and energize us, causing us to smile and grow and love.

CULTIVATING HOPE

Emptying Out the Locker

For two-and-a-half decades my exercise regimen has involved tri-weekly basketball games. Several colleagues and I started a "noon hoops" tradition at George Fox University when I was a new assistant professor in the 1980s—a tradition that is still going strong every Monday, Wednesday, and Friday. And during my 13-year sojourn at Wheaton College, I started an early morning basketball tradition there with some faculty and staff colleagues. (I like to build things, including basketball traditions.) Basketball has been a way of life for me, an activity that causes me to reflect gratefully when others talk about their difficulty finding enjoyable ways to exercise.

About a year ago I noticed—with Lisa's help—how often basketball-related injuries were altering my life. The injuries have piled up over the years: ankle sprains, a groin pull, back spasms, a blow to the throat that took my singing voice away, sore knees and feet, a deviated septum, and so on. Injuries are part of the game, but now they come more often, causing me to wonder about the wisdom of continuing. Lisa is pretty sure I'm foolish to try to keep up with 20-somethings on the court anyway; and as hard as it is to admit, I think she may be right. I have played less and less over the past six months, and not at all in the last several weeks. And it's helping. Last week I almost fell off a ladder while painting a hen house. When I could tell gravity was winning the battle, I decided to jump rather than fall. My four-foot downward jump caused me no knee pain at all and reminded me that my knees are recovering from all those years of basketball.

Yesterday brought a poignant end to my basketball-playing days as I went into the familiar-smelling locker room, opened my Ace Hardware padlock for the last time and emptied the locker.

I have often imagined death as a final gate, a passage to something beyond. The passing will be frightening, no doubt, but hope lies on the other side, too, just as hope has filled my life this side of the gate. Yesterday while emptying that locker, I realized that aging—moving towards death—brings not one gate to pass through, but many as I pass from one way of living to another. But each gate provides opportunities for hope to flourish amidst loss. Perhaps kindling this hope is the great test of aging—a gentle grace that persists and permeates the passages of life and death.

Immediately after cleaning out the basketball locker, I strolled to the George Fox undergraduate chapel where a worship band led the community in praise choruses. "Your grace is enough, your grace is enough, your grace is enough for me." Though I can't sing much or well because of that decade-old blow to my throat on the basketball court, I let these words wash over me. My mind went back to the locker room where I had just loaded my black Nikes into a tattered green gym bag. "Your grace is enough." And the words drew me forward, imagining the gateways before me—losing my parents to death, increasing struggles with health concerns in years ahead, losing relevance to my students, getting a hearing aid, giving up farming, watching Lisa pass though that final gate perhaps—or her watching me. In all this a quiet wisdom resonated with the words sung by a thousand tongues, most of them owned by 18- to 22-year-olds: "Your grace is enough for me."

May it be so. God, grant me the grace to keep seeing hope on both sides of every gate.

Lisa and I walk together for exercise. Most days we take a brisk walk up the hill near Fern Creek, breathing vigorously because of the incline, greeting the horses and sheep along the way, noticing the color of spring, ending at the top of the hill where we encounter the "Winery Closed" sign. We offer some well-worn winery joke because there is no winery at the top of the hill—just protective property owners who don't want trespassers.

"I can't believe how often this winery is closed," I say.

"We really should call ahead so we don't take this walk for nothing," Lisa replies.

Then we walk back down the hill, greet the sheep and horses again, appreciate the gorgeous view of Mount Hood on clear days, and end up back at Fern Creek feeling energized and refreshed.

Giving up basketball is sad and difficult, but it is also good, opening new possibilities of health and hope for this aging soul. Hope is a gentle grace. May it be evident and abundant as I navigate the passages of life.

Lisa

Saying Grace

During our sophomore year of high school, when Mark's and my love was especially young, we'd meet up after school and sit on a cement bench that overlooked the football field. We'd read a psalm together, pray, and then kiss goodbye. I'd head home or to my job as a typesetter at Litho Graphics, and Mark went to football or basketball practice. I cherished our innocent kisses, counting them on my fingers and then my toes. That year for Christmas Mark gave me a pocket-sized leather-bound New Testament and Psalms. His inscription read: *May the strength of our relationship depend on God, because the strength of God is one thing we can depend on.*

Thirty-five years later our love is less young and our faith more old. Mark and I have shared the tasks of making a home, living a life. I'm as likely to slip behind the steering wheel as Mark is when we drive somewhere; we shared in the caretaking of our children; and do the same now with our grandchildren. Mark is far better at cleaning the floors than I am, and I at scouring the kitchen. Neither of us particularly likes cleaning bathrooms or windows which means they get pretty dirty before we attend to them, usually together. Some tasks fall more into traditional roles. I do more of the meal planning, cooking, and baking—although, except for Christmas cookies, Mark makes all the cookies and these days all the pies. I wash and dry more laundry; Mark does almost all the lawn mowing, gutter cleaning, and wood splitting.

In recent years the act of saying grace before dinner defaults to Mark, and he graciously accepts the responsibility. That he does so symbolizes how Mark is a steady rock for my faith. We both have had—and continue to have—questions about Christianity, the religion we claim as ours. But the questions have never shaken Mark's decision to choose faith, to believe in a loving Creator that made the earth-shattering decision to become human and live among us, fully experiencing our humanity while showing us the face of God.

When my questions become troubling, Mark's faith becomes my constant. And it's *not* because we pray and have devotions together (we do the former occasionally and the latter almost never). Mark is my constant as I bear witness to his life of faith. I see him seek God and strive to respond to God's love by pursuing justice, extending mercy, and walking humbly in the day in and day out choices about what he eats, buys, how he loves our neighbors near and far, and our children, parents, and me. His commitment to our Quaker church strengthens mine.

He will take uncomfortable stands. When buying the ham for his department's Christmas gathering fell to us, he insisted on buying one from a pig allowed to range outside rather than a less expensive one raised in an inhumane CAFO (Concentrated Animal Feeding Operations). He does this because his faith requires him to notice and love God's world and to take care that God's creatures are treated humanely—even the ones we plan to eat. His faith sometimes leads him into uncomfortable places—like the homeless shelter where we volunteer as overnight hosts one night a month, which is far outside his (and my) comfort zone. Mark stands by his belief that Jesus was fully human and fully God even as he knows some find it incredulous than an intelligent man would hold such a myth as truth. He holds it with grace and humility.

Mark's unwavering faith is a comfort to me—not because he does not ask hard questions, but because of the simplicity of belief that comes from making a decision to believe and then striving to live consistently from that choice.

Witnessing such a life grounds my faith in hope.

Mark

Strawberry Fields Forever

It's late October and I'm already thinking about how good a June Oregon strawberry tastes. When living in Illinois we occasionally tried the strawberries available at the Jewel grocery store down the street, but were inevitably disappointed with the imported-from-someplace-where-it's-warm varieties. A fresh, local Oregon strawberry is a thing to behold: bright red, large fruit, brimming with a burst of sweet flavor. Not all strawberries taste the same. We grow Benton, Hood, Rainier, and Tristar berries. Each has unique flavor, different times of ripening, and varying lengths of production. Even at the end of October we are still harvesting a few Tristars. They are plenty good, but nothing matches the flavor of June-bearing cultivars.

Like every species we encounter, strawberries love to reproduce. Last year we planted 12 Rainier and 24 Hood plants, and after producing their flavorful fruit they started putting out runners. Runners are long stems that shoot out from the mother plant and take root wherever they can find soil. Rather than just chopping them off and throwing them away, I decided to redeem this year's runners and build a bigger strawberry patch for next year. Lisa doesn't exactly understand my love of strawberries and my eagerness to enlarge our bounty, but she nodded her head sympathetically and watched me till a 100 x 16 foot area, dig up a few hundred runners (June-bearing plants go crazy with runners), and plant what I hope to be next year's berry patch. She thinks I'm a driven individual and feels some measure of pity for me, which I do not fully understand.

Runners are vulnerable things, often small, with a nascent root structure and no track record of surviving. I chopped them off from their mothers, plopped them in the ground, watered them for a couple weeks, and begged them to live as Lisa and I headed off for an eight-day vacation in New England. Upon returning, many dozens of brown strawberry plants appeared dead from thirst. I grieved a bit, and then I went out to hoe between rows and greet the few survivors. Hoeing is a bit of a euphemism; crawling would be another way of describing it as I regularly descend to hands and knees to pull out weeds living close to the plants. While down among them, I saw again how vibrant and enthusiastic and abundant life can be.

In the midst of those thirsty brown strawberry plants—which I had taken for dead—I discovered tiny bundles of small green foliage ready to erupt. What looked like a crop failure will turn out to be a lush field of berries in a year and three-quarters. Lisa and I could have berry fights two

Junes from now if we were prone to such a thing. Instead, we will feast in spring's bounty and give pounds and pounds of berries to our CSA subscribers.

It's strange that tiny green leaves would cause tears to well in a grown man's eyes, but that's exactly what happened. My mind went back to the difficult years of marriage, long ago. I recalled heated exchanges, words that should have never been spoken, deep fear and anxiety and anger. This went on for years—four of them by my count, and even more by Lisa's. But life is a tenacious thing, or at least it was for us. As if in cadence with some grand rhythm of grace built into the fabric of creation, Lisa and I began to see hope sprouting amidst the decay. Her eyes became kinder, and I think mine did, too. We began listening again, and dreaming of our future. Laughter and safety returned. Our love began to flourish once more. It still takes my breath away, filling my soul with grateful praise.

A marriage full of life blesses husband and wife, and more. I ponder how the love that Lisa and I share blesses our children and grandchildren, siblings and parents, friends and colleagues, and perhaps even the critters in the place we live.

Fern Creek is a peaceful place where the deer wander up to our back porch, the birds sing, the honeybees and hummingbirds prosper, and the squirrels frolic. Our friends and students observe this to be a place of peace. Perhaps this comes, in part, from the verdant life that springs forth from two souls living a life of gratitude.

Soon we'll have an abundance of berries. Maybe I'll throw one at Lisa when she accuses me of being driven. I suppose we'll put them on our morning cereal; slice and eat them for lunch; enjoy smoothies, berry crisps and pies; freeze them for the winter; and still give most of them away.

A Call Toward Life

We ordered 25 chicks from a hatchery in Texas that arrived at the Newberg Post Office on Friday morning. I got a call at 7 a.m. from a postal worker who said they had arrived at 4 a.m., but he didn't think I'd want to be awakened that early. (Side note: my dear husband went in to Portland to be with Junie so I could be here for the arrival and first care of these little chicks. I love that he is comfortable enough as a grandpa to provide care for our six-month-old granddaughter by himself, a task we have been sharing during this sabbatical year.)

I wish I had let the post office know to call me as soon as a box labeled "live poultry" arrived. It's unnatural to hatch chickens in January. Hens know keeping their babies warm in winter is challenging, so their bodies slow down or stop producing eggs until spring.

That means baby chicks are hard to come by unless you order them from someone making a business of hatching chicks year around. We only wanted 18, but chicks get shipped in groups of 25 so their collective body heat, inconsequential though it is, will keep them warm during the 48 hours or so it takes to get them resettled. Chicks don't need to eat or drink for a couple of days (which makes this whole shipping chicks thing possible) because they're nourished by the yoke which they finish drawing into their stomachs just before hatching out. But they arrive thirsty and cold, and this particular box of chicks sat out on the receiving dock in Newberg for three hours.

After opening the box I saw that a couple were already dead and several more looked iffy. In the warmth of our kitchen nook I began taking them out one at a time, dipping their beaks into warm sugar water and setting them in a warmed bin bedded with pine shavings covered with a paper towel. They chirped uncertainly, accepted the baptismal of sorts and fell into a sleepy haze of warmth as I set them in their new home. I had to re-dunk some of them the first couple of hours, wanting to be sure they knew where to find the water their bodies craved.

Three more died within that first day, unable to turn back toward life. Somewhere in the first hour I counted and realized only 20 chicks had been shipped, explaining the unusually high mortality rate. I felt irresponsible for choosing to have newly hatched chicks shipped at such an unnatural time of year. "Next time," I decided, "I'll incubate and hatch them out here."

I justified my choice to send for chicks in January because of the greater good we're attempting to do as farmers.

We have a small flock that spends the winter doing magic in one of our two gardens, and I wanted a second flock to do the same in the other garden. And if our chicks arrived in January, they will be laying by the time our Community Supported Agriculture starts in June. That way we can offer eggs to our subscribers who want them, helping ease some of the dependency on eggs coming from factory farms where hens exist in truly miserable, unnatural conditions.

I'm monitoring the chicks' health, changing the water several times a day because they like to stand on the edge and poop in it, working the heat lamp to keep the temperature around 90 degrees, and cleaning up pasty butts. Pasty butts are nasty on several counts, but for a chick they're nasty because a vent (the dual-purpose defecation and egg laying channel) blocked with dried poop prevents further pooping. You can imagine the problem. So I pick them up, stick their rear end into a yogurt container filled with warm water, hold them there for a minute and then work loose the dried poop plug. Not a pleasant task, but at least it's a small one.

Part of living is taking care of the needs of the young, sick, wounded, and dying. I contemplated these things as I nurtured the surviving chicks, calling them back toward life when they were cold and slipping toward death.

We call each other toward life all the time. Mothers and fathers do it when they feed their families with food that grows and sustains muscles, bones, hearts, and kidneys. Last night Mark and I went to Portland to watch *Forks over Knifes*—a pre-release viewing of a documentary that claims we could turn around our skyrocketing rates of diabetes, obesity, strokes, heart disease, and some cancers if we would feed our children and ourselves more plants and whole foods and less sugars, fats, and animal products. We found it compelling, but then, we're mostly members of the choir on that anthem already.

I committed to life with Mark in sickness and in health the day I married him. None of us who make that commitment know all that it might entail. We don't know if we will care for one who no longer recognizes us or who may become incapacitated and dependent on us far too early in life. But we also committed to health—to calling each other toward life as we worked toward a lifestyle that fostered physical, emotional, and spiritual well-being. At times I've attended too compulsively to diet and exercise regimes, letting it consume my best energy. But I also don't want to error on the side of attending too little, trusting food manufacturers to sell only healthy food, and relying on drugs and doctors to make me well when my lifestyle makes me sick.

We call each other to life and hope when we stay open to learning, recognizing our best teachers might be those less vulnerable to fads and new drugs (which may mean digging up wisdom known by our great-grandmothers). Maybe if we ate more plants and whole foods like people do in Asia and used our bodies more functionally like people do in much of the majority world, we'd have less obesity, diabetes, and heart disease. Scads of research on the matter suggest this is true.

Now, a week later, the surviving 15 chicks test their wings as they hop around the bin chasing each other, working out the pecking order, eating chick feed, and drinking water. Still they collapse together in heaps when they lay down to sleep, drawing warmth from each other's fluffy little bodies.

Mark

Growing Old

After a night interrupted a dozen times or so with a sharp sciatica pain, I felt pleased to see the old digital clock approaching 8:00 as I reached my final awakening—much later than our normal rising and only possible on a sabbatical year. Lisa got out of bed first, rustling the sheets on her side of the bed as I said, "Happy anniversary." Today is our thirty-second. Surprisingly, she didn't respond. She's never been the type to offer silence in response to my words—even when annoyed at me—and I couldn't think of any reason for her to be annoyed anyway. It puzzled me. A moment later I said, "I think that generally receives some sort of reply." Still nothing. I concluded that her ears are just not what they used to be, even as I admitted to myself that my hearing is worse than hers.

Twenty minutes later, standing in the kitchen, watching the oatmeal cook, I recounted the conversation, expecting

Lisa to feel embarrassed. Instead, she told me her version. She began the morning by saying, "Happy anniversary" as she climbed out of bed. Apparently, I didn't hear her.

I said, "Happy anniversary," which she took as a reply. Then a minute later I mumbled something about not getting a reply, which confused her just enough to stay silent. We chuckled, both concluding that my hearing really is worse than hers. The audiologist tells me my hearing isn't bad enough for a hearing aid yet. Lisa thinks I should get a second opinion. She's happy to be the one to offer it.

There are, more or less, three good things about growing old (which pale a bit in comparison to the list of good things about being young, but they are still good to remember). One is that growing old beats the alternative: dying. Two is that some people, sometimes, take you more seriously when you're old, as if wisdom really does come with age. Three: some of us have the privilege of growing old alongside someone else. This is one of my life's great blessings and will someday be a blessing recounted in death by one of us.

We were young once—before hearing loss and sciatica and wrinkles and white hair. Those were good years, too, with laughter and friendship and hard work. We raised three daughters together, loving and praying for and sacrificing for them more than they will ever know, though it never felt onerous. We built careers and professional identities, mentored students, worked through some tough times in our marriage. The anniversaries kept rolling around every December, and as some of our friends lost their marriages, we resolved to hold on tighter to ours, to celebrate each passing year as a gift. It's hard to know which day of which year we suddenly recognized that we are growing old, but it felt abrupt and came too soon.

Here's a conversation we've had several dozen times in the last few years:

Mark: We got old, Lisa. How did it happen?

Lisa: We just kept on living.

And so we have, and we hope to for many more years. And not just living as in passing the days toward a date with death, but living an abundant life. To be sure, there are bulging disks and hearing loss, but the main theme of our growing old is joy and abundance and gratitude to God.

We have spoken on Christian college campuses about hopes and fears of marriage, but what do two people who married when Jimmy Carter was President know about marriage in the twenty-first century? So we've surveyed students before speaking on their campuses and have now collected data from 3,100 students. One of the highest hopes today's college students report for marriage is "growing old with someone." So there we stand at the chapel podium, talking with the barely- and not-even-20-something students in the audience, all of us wanting the same thing, all of us wanting to grow old alongside another. At the end of our survey, we include an open-ended comment box about hopes in marriage. One Wheaton College man responded this way:

> Kisses and lingerie and carrying my wife;
> laughing a lot, enjoying life together, encouraging
> one another, waking up beside each other,
> not being alone at night, memorizing Psalms
> together, teaching piano lessons, raising a family,
> visiting grandkids, visiting friends and family,
> hiking in mountains, cuddling up by the fire,
> someone to worship at church with, someone
> to serve and give everything I have to, someone's
> feet I can rub, someone to pray with, someone
> to cry with and carry each other's burdens
> in a safe committed relationship.

When speaking at Wheaton, Lisa and I read this quote in chapel on a Monday and had calls and e-mails all week from women who wanted to meet this guy. We patiently reminded each inquirer that the survey was anonymous; we didn't know who provided such a lovely quote about marriage. One woman didn't give up—she asked us to read her name in chapel on Friday so this anonymous guy would know she wanted to meet him.

Another Wheaton woman wrote on her questionnaire: "I am hoping that, in approximately 53 years, we'll still like each other enough to start smoking cigars together on the porch every night (because, seriously, by that age, who cares about lung cancer?)." She may be wrong about when people give up caring about cancer, but she is right about wanting 53 years or more with one's partner.

This aging together that Lisa and I know is what young people yearn for. We all want the privilege of living long enough to joke about hearing loss. We all want a thirty-second anniversary, and then a fifty-third. Those of us who encounter such a thing are deeply blessed.

Lisa

The Children's Farm

When Ada, my friend and one of our CSA subscribers, picked up her crate of vegetables, she asked if I dreaded or enjoyed pick up days. "I like these days very much," I said. As an introvert it surprises me that visiting with our subscribers brings me joy. I especially like subscribers who bring their children—children inevitably inclined to explore Fern Creek's forest, creek, gardens, and especially the hen houses.

Today was the second week of our second CSA season, and this time around we are growing food for 13 families. Since the cool wet spring has meant less of everything than we hoped (except greens, onions, and radishes!), the first week everyone received a tomato plant with a little bag of our home-brewed fertilizer and a link to my blog where I outline tips for successful transplanting. This week I made everyone a small loaf of sunflower wheat bread sweetened with honey from our hives. Besides, I've found baking as well as growing food for appreciative and grateful people to be deeply satisfying. If we can't give them actual food from the gardens, we'll bake them some and give them a plant that holds the hope of food to come.

Today when Angie pulled up in her red Subaru, five-year-old Luke and three-year-old Jack tumbled out of the car and came up to the courtyard to see what food the crates held this week and mostly, I think, to get permission to go visit the hens. "Last week I had to drag them here," Angie said. "This week they kept asking, 'When do we get to go to our farm again?' *Our* farm. Isn't that great? They don't usually take to a place or get so talkative with strangers as quickly as they have here."

My face and heart both smiled and I asked the boys if they wanted to go feed the hens some of their special treat mix I save for CSA days. On the way Angie told me her husband thought Fern Creek eggs were the best eggs he'd ever eaten—the whites standing up so firm and the yolks deep yellow/orange and the taste—mmm, so good. I carried the bucket and scoop and we all went into the yard where the boys took turns tossing corn, wheat, sunflower seeds, peanuts, lentils, and oats to our hens who, in the presence of such a feast, sometimes tolerate petting.

Luke talked about chickens in kindergarten and he understood that fertilized eggs turned into chicks. After eating a couple of their eggs last week he told his mom, "We could fertilize some of these and then have our own chickens!"

"Except that we can't fertilize them," Angie said.

"Yes we can. Remember, the farmer gave us fertilizer last week!" he replied with enthusiasm.

I love the workings of children's curious minds—children wanting to understand how pieces of the world fit together, how to untangle earth's mysteries and engage them. I love how children listen when we don't realize it, absorbing information and also values: like respect for land, chickens, and bees, and love of food grown naturally from a farmer just over the hill and down the road.

From the chicken yard we walked through the forest to the giraffe tree with Luke leading the way. "We're in the forest now," he said with a touch of awe and gentle respect as we left the sunny field and entered the cool shade of the woods. He gently swooshed ferns out of his way as he forged forward.

Their delight feeds my soul. I want to be more childlike, able to touch and feel the goodness of God in the feathery softness of a hen's back warmed by the sun, or from the cushiony moss growing on a tree that nearly broke, but survived, yielding to a giraffe-like appearance that created a perfect saddle seat for contemplating life. Jack, Luke, Noah, Malachi, Connor, Kate, Micah, Henry, Charlie, and Auden are children eating from the abundance of Fern Creek this season. Their parents are connecting them to food in powerful ways—allowing them to see that food comes from dirt—not a box—grown on vines, bushes, stalks, and trees.

Their delight renews my hope for the generation to come.

Mark

Grace in the Kitchen

Like life itself, CSA days start fast and end slow.

The flurry of morning harvesting gives way to midday sorting. Most of the fruits and vegetables are Grade A, which lands them in crates for distribution to our subscribers. A few are Grade B, meaning there is a split in the potato or cabbage, or some extra holes in the lettuce, or the berries are smaller than usual. Grade B food goes to those helping us harvest or we keep it ourselves. Afternoon brings conversation as we interact with subscribers coming to Fern Creek to pick up their food. We are tired when evening comes, though a deep sense of satisfaction wraps itself around our fatigue, reminding us of how very good this day has been.

Today we began by harvesting marionberries, blueberries, raspberries, and the ever surprising Tristar strawberries. Tristars bear all summer, long after the Benton, Ranier, and Hood strawberries have given up for the season—a nice metaphor for aging souls. We harvest kale, broccoli, lettuce, and green and red cabbage. Lisa harvests beets while I pull and rinse onions and dig potatoes. She gathers herbs, as always, because I'm likely to confuse thyme with oregano—or just about any herb with any other one. I find it much easier to identify a potato than a mint leaf.

Subscribers come and go along with the afternoon. So does our daughter Megan Anna and son-in-law Luke, leaving us to enjoy our granddaughter Grace for a couple hours as we plan and prepare supper with our portion of Grade B food.

We place Grace on the counter where she tries out her precocious 13-month-old vocabulary, snacks on potato and cabbage, and plays with the bottle containing rice vinegar. I chop and season my way toward a cabbage salad as Lisa crafts another with lettuce, beets, Oregon hazelnuts, and feta cheese.

"Do we have any sweet onions?" Lisa asks.

"I think some of those Walla Walla sweets are ready now," I say. A moment later Grace and I are back in the garden looking for our most mature sweet onion. She carries it back in the house as I carry her.

"Herego," says Grace as we deliver the onion to Lisa.

Later I ask Lisa if we have any cilantro, so she kindly heads to the herb garden to harvest cilantro along with the mint and basil I need for the dressing.

Our preparations yield all sorts of vegetable scraps, so Grace and I head back outside to the lower hen house where we delight the hens with our Grade C scraps. On our way back to the house, her parents show up. Lisa and I bid goodbye to our dear granddaughter and put the finishing touches on our supper.

We set the table outside on the courtyard where shade mutes the early evening July sun. As is our custom, we bow and say grace, thanking God for the abundance of this life and the goodness of creation. Another of our customs is to note how much of our meal is local. We groan in delight as we taste the berries from our gardens, then again as we enjoy a rather remarkable cabbage salad and the lettuce and beet salad topped with hazelnuts from a farmer down the road. We enjoy a local Pinot Gris which came from a barter we made with a vineyard owner last winter who needed the tractor blade we posted on Craigslist.

As we enjoy this Grade A feast from our Grade B produce, we ponder the origins of the feta, olive oil, sesame oil, rice vinegar, Dijon mustard, salt, and pepper from who-knows-where. We offer words of thanks for farmers and artisans everywhere—for those who grow sesame seeds and age cheese and know how to make rice vinegar. Our conversation meanders as we discuss the fullness of the day, local food, this good life together. A comfortable silence settles over us, then renewed conversation, then more silence.

The sun continues its relentless westward journey toward dusk. Lisa and I sit as two contended souls, knowing the end of this very good day is near.

CULTIVATING HUMILITY AND OPENNESS

Lisa

Apprenticing Life

Our final sabbatical building project is a big one. Bigger even than building hen houses (we built two this year), or a gazebo with a brick fire pit in the middle and a bridge to get to it. We're calling our new project *The Potting Shed*. It will be part green house and part pottery studio, a place where pots and vessels of all sorts will be created out of clay.

The front third will contain windows from ceiling to about waist high and the back two-thirds framed and sided. A potter's wheel and stool will welcome throwers and surround them with natural light and a view of the forest as they throw. We thought about calling the room *The Dirt Room* since clay is made from dirt and plants grow out of dirt, but that doesn't convey the respect we have for dirt, nor the sense of peace and calm for ruffled souls that we hope the room holds. So *The Potting Shed* it is.

Maybe the vision for sharing this space is naïve. We will know soon enough. But many of our projects begin with the sort of creativity that a bit of naivety allows.

Naïve or not, we like blending these two tasks, where we can be apprentices of life and practice creating, reflecting God's creativity whether throwing pots or cultivating life. Both offer reminders that we are made in the image of God—apprentices who can create, cultivate, and nourish life with our work.

We're attaching *The Potting Shed* to the side of the house, so we're matching siding and brickwork. Mark and I have dug out the slope, mixed cement in our old red wheelbarrow for the footings, built a half-wall with cement blocks, and are now bricking over the outside of the cement blocks. Mark has a good eye for level, although he still uses a level to check himself. We'd been working on perpendicular walls and every so often he'd check out mine and say (patiently, mind you), "You are getting high on the back end again," as he tapped down the back of my brick. I couldn't see it. I still can't see it. But set my little orange torpedo level on the brick and sure enough—the off-center yellow bubble tells me the end is high.

My bricks need to be checked for level on about three dimensions, unlike Mark who only has to check his on one dimension. This much I know is true: I can't always trust what I'm seeing. So if I want to lay straight bricks, I need some objective measure to help me see what I cannot.

I learned the same lesson throwing pots. My pots—however nicely shaped, trimmed, and glazed—lilted to one side when set on the table. The foot was inevitably thicker on one side than the other and I couldn't figure out why that kept happening. Eventually (four pots or so later) it occurred to me that the top rims of my pots were not level, so when I turned them upside down on the wheel to trim the bottoms, the uneven rim got replicated on the foot. Once I figured that out, I started correcting for the crookedness I could not see by using the torpedo level and bits of clay to shim my pots before trimming them. A better strategy yet is to trim up unevenness in the lip when I'm still throwing the pot.

I'm learning to appreciate tools and the expertise of others who have practiced art and life longer, or differently, than I have. They help provide objectivity and clarity as I work at the art of living well so that I don't have to figure everything out on my own. My teachers and guides help with all sorts of things—like how to support my adult children, plant sweet potatoes, introduce a new chicken to an existing flock, or respond to the killing of Osama bin Laden.

I'm learning it's okay to *not* trust my perception—even though it's in vogue to trust our guts to know a thing. Checking out my perception against some other measures or expertise doesn't make me weak. Maybe in fact, it means I am finally becoming a humble apprentice. And a wiser steward.

Mark

When the Clouds Roll In

Yesterday we enjoyed a 77-degree October day in Northwest Oregon with sun warming the soil and encouraging the remaining pole beans, cantaloupe, cucumbers, and tomatoes. Today the clouds are rolling in.

People say it rains a lot in Oregon, which is only partly true. From late October to late May, it does. From June to mid-October, it almost never rains. These are glorious days for sun-starved Oregonians. We walk, bike, hike, kayak, swim, socialize, and eat outdoors, soaking in the warmth of the season. In late June and early July, the morning sun streams through our bedroom window by 5 a.m., lighting and warming the landscape until almost 10 p.m., and we love being outdoors as many of the 17 intervening hours as possible.

Summer fades to autumn, and soon the pumpkins, apples, hazelnuts, and grapes are all harvested and the clouds start forming in the western horizon. Temperatures drop, days shorten, and rain looms. We clean our gutters and brace ourselves for what comes next.

It's not that rain is all bad. Those of us raised in Oregon find comfort in its familiarity and rhythm. It moistens the dry land, then drenches it, making the winter landscape both muddy and verdant. Oregon precipitation falls as gentle mist more often than not. I don't own an umbrella, nor do I need one, because our rain is far different than a Midwest downpour. Despite the rain, Oregonians still walk and hike and kayak and socialize outdoors on mild winter days. Life goes on. One could even say that life is better because of the rain, knowing that our rain in the Willamette Valley means a heavy snowpack in the Cascade Range and ample supplies of fresh water—raging rapids and brimming aquifers—for the coming summer months. Still, the rain takes its toll. Valuable minerals leach out of garden soil, cars rust, gutters leak, and eventually even the hardiest of Oregonians begins yearning for the clear skies of summer.

I recall a week of childhood seemingly spoiled by rain. My friends and I spent weeks planning a "spring sports tournament" to be held over spring vacation. We were to move from one friend's house to another, playing outdoor basketball, football, soccer, and wiffle ball. For a country kid living seven miles from town, this sports-filled week represented the sort of fun and social connection that I yearned for. I counted down the days for spring break, dreaming every night about hitting homeruns and scoring touchdowns, and "giving five" to my teammates (this was before the days of "high fives"). But that particular Oregon March overflowed with rain. I spent my spring break sitting on an avocado green shag carpet, surrounded with piles of baseball cards, looking out the plate glass window from the living room, hoping the clouds would soon clear. They didn't.

All these years later, I still wish the clouds wouldn't have rolled in that March week in the early 1970s. But they did, and I suspect that disappointment helped forge some good qualities in me that have helped more than a week of sports-filled fun might have. Most of us want to be patient, resilient, persistent people, but the only way these qualities can be formed is by facing disappointment and struggle. I wish there were another way for strong character to form in human souls, but there is not. If we want to be strong enough to press against the rain and the wind, we must have inclement weather in order to build and prove our endurance and strength. Each of us can scroll through the annals of our lives and find disappointments a thousand times more poignant than a canceled spring sports tournament—broken relationships, shattered expectations, times of struggle and deep despair. And let's not be Pollyannaish about it—tragedies are *tragic*. We cannot twist them into good things with some poetic maneuvering. I recall several hard years early in marriage when Lisa and I both thought our joy of being together was forever lost. We were wrong—both in the ways we treated each other back then and in our pessimism about the future. In all the ugliness and awfulness of life's struggles we often see the redemptive presence of a faithful God whispering hope in the rubble of ruin. With this divine whisper comes a reminder not only that rain builds character, but also that a brighter day is coming.

When the sunny days of spring return, what glorious celebration of life ensues. Trees bud, birds frolic and sing, and new life springs forth from the earth. Warmth and light stream through our souls and brighten our smiles.

Lisa

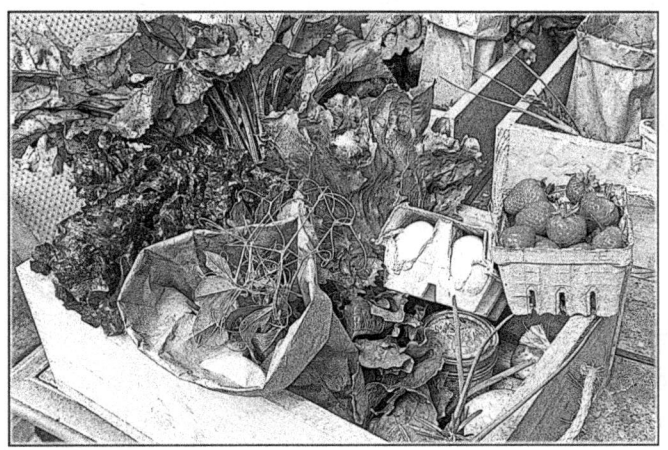

A Waste of a Worry

At five our daughter Sarah showed signs of being a worrier. She fretted about not falling asleep; worried that the house would burn down or that I would die while she was away at kindergarten; that she would *fail* kindergarten or her swim lessons (that one turned out to be true—my fault, not hers); or that the family would be late for church, which happened rarely, but enough to merit some measure of fretting.

    I always wanted to create the calm Sunday mornings of my childhood, a before-church experience that included homemade coffee cake and eggs for breakfast and praying together before we headed off to church. We seldom managed it. The coffee cake became a regular part of Sunday morning for a while, though I'm embarrassed to admit Costco muffins replaced the coffee cake somewhere during our daughters' adolescent years.

One Sunday morning when Sarah was about five, we were scurrying around getting the five of us breakfasted, hair and teeth brushed, dressed, shoes on and buckled, and into the car. We made it on time and as we slid into the pew Sarah said, "Well, *that* was a waste of a worry." The phrase stuck, and we've used it liberally for the last 25 years.

This week we started our second season as CSA farmers. The ocean-atmosphere phenomena known as La Nina that made last spring unseasonably cool and rainy hadn't quite run its course, meaning we had another cold, wet spring this year. This year seemed even worse than last, dooming our crates to be especially sparse. We had worried last year, and since everything had turned out okay we had hoped to worry less this time around. But worry we did. This year's sugar and snap peas had just begun to blossom and the kohlrabi and broccoli weren't even close to ready—vegetables we included the first week of last year, even if just a small sampling of them. We had hoped for strawberries to make up for it, but the robins took bites out of what few strawberries did ripen and it would take a few weeks before enough would be ready.

My only consolation was knowing that no other CSA farm would be doing any better, but that's a small consolation when Walmart, Safeway, and Grocery Outlet displayed all these vegetables in bounteous quantities—good looking ones without any holes left by hungry slugs. I worried that our subscribers would think they were getting cheated, that they would want their money back, and worst of all, that Mark and I were incompetent farmers—professors posing as farmers.

But it was a waste of a worry. We had two luscious heads of lettuce for each crate (a blush butter romaine and sunset red loose leaf), a big and mostly beetle-bite-free bunch of radishes, beautiful bunching onions, a bag of spinach, arugula and (wilted) mustard greens, a very small bag of new potatoes, some chives, rosemary, and a head of garlic left over from last year. My dear mother-in-law offered rhubarb and asparagus from her abundantly producing garden, and we gave everyone a potted heirloom Cherokee Purple tomato plant—extras we had started from seed—with some of our organic home-brewed fertilizer. And subscribers who signed up by March 1 (which was most of them) received a cookbook perfect for using seasonal vegetables—either *Simply in Season* or *From Asparagus to Zucchini.* Those who opted to add either a half dozen or a dozen eggs received an assortment of white, brown, tan, and the occasional blue egg. I topped off the crate with my enlightening (even if a tad apologetic) weekly newsletter, complete with recipes and tips, like how *not* to be surprised by little white pellets in their lettuce (our safe-to-eat-though-I-don't-recommend-it organic slug bait), or the occasional surviving slug. This just goes to show that organic methods, while safe, are not quite as effective as conventional pesticides, which are nasty for a reason.

All that to say, subscribers seemed excited with their first crates. Several of the new folks took tours. I walked a woman and her two young sons up to see the chickens where we found three eggs in their nesting boxes—a fun discovery for the boys. I showed them the paths into the woods. As we walked past the picnic tables and down toward the gazebo, I could tell they were already making plans to return with shoes for proper exploration and an appetite for adventure.

I like harvest/pick up days. It's the day we share what we do with those who have entrusted themselves to us for the summer. Their trust and enthusiasm inspires confidence. Next week I'll bake small loaves of honey/sunflower seed wheat bread and tuck it into their crates along with a small jar of honey from last year's harvest. It's a way to say thank you for choosing to belong to our CSA family.

Besides, it'll waylay any concern I have that next week's crate may still be a bit light on the produce side. But I refuse to continue to fret about being thought of as a pitiful farmer and provider of vegetables. Our subscribers know the food they get from us is influenced by the weather we get from God. It would be a waste of a worry. Instead I will be grateful for dirt that provides food and for people who support our efforts to grow it.

Mark

Being a Man

Because I'm an ambitious sort, and because we turned away potential subscribers to our CSA last year, Lisa and I decided to expand our farming area. Now that mid-January is here, it's time to pull out the hand-powered auger and start digging holes for the new deer fence (deer are great to look at, but they like vegetables too much to give them free rein). Lisa makes sure the post is plumb and fills in dirt while I dig the next hole.

The only snafu has to do with vocabulary. After Lisa puts the dirt back in the hole, one of us pounds the dirt around the post with the handle end of the shovel. This process, called *tamping,* assures dirt is compacted and firm so that the post will survive Oregon rain. Yesterday Lisa referred to this as *tapping* the dirt. It's amazing the difference one letter can make. Calling this process *tapping* somehow offends my manhood, reducing something one does with a shovel in the mud to something that can be done with manicured fingernails on a countertop.

Our little vocabulary problem brought to mind some fragmented memory that still reverberates in my brain 40 years later, though I cannot fully recall the event or the circumstances. My grandfather is there—a lifelong farmer, strong as can be—and my father, too. They are teaching me to install fence posts, telling me the importance of tamping the dirt. I'm too small to put enough muscle into it, so they let me practice tamping for a while before finishing the job with their adult strength. I remember wishing I could be old and strong, like they were.

The memory is so trivial that it doesn't require prime-time space in my brain's memory storage. But today, as I was tamping down dirt, the memory came visiting, causing me to wonder when I became a man. Of course I have always been male, but when did I become a man? I pondered this for a moment before realizing that if manhood is marked by strength, then there will soon be a day when my manhood leaves me. Even now I find the physicality of digging holes and planting posts to be more exhausting than I remember it to be in days past. It caused a moment of panic, thinking I am finally a man now and then realizing my manhood is already passing me by.

As much as I am drawn to images of manhood that involve hitting people on the gridiron or pumping iron or doing pushups, those have never defined me particularly well. In my life manhood is closely tied to personhood—to being a listener with a tender heart, a father whose primary strength is compassion, and a partner to a woman who has more inner fortitude than I will ever have. Being a man meant sacrificing some of my professional ambitions when Lisa opted to pursue a graduate degree. Manliness meant stepping up and learning how to cook as social roles began shifting in the 1980s. It meant encouraging Lisa and our three daughters to find voice and confidence in a society where women are still sometimes marginalized. I take hope in this, both because manhood thus defined is a bit countercultural—and I like that sort of bravado—and because I can hold on to this sort of manhood for years to come, maybe even for a few more decades.

Still, I like muscles and strength and working in the mud. Almost getting stuck in the mud in my four-wheel drive pickup last December provided a surge of manly adrenalin. But I don't want to confuse being a man with the stereotypes of manliness offered in commercials or on billboards on the expressway. Might and virility have their place, but they are as fleeting as life itself. When the day comes for tamping to turn to tapping, I pray for the grace to see that my strength is not so much in the power I exert over the world around me, but in the willingness to accept my limitations, to exercise the gifts of mercy and kindness that don't require young muscles, and to support and celebrate family and friends.

Lisa

On Dandelions

As a high school sophomore I stuck my chin out to the world and announced that I loved dandelions. I saw beauty in the delicate yellow flower tinged with purple that turns into a perfect seed ball ready to go wherever the wind sends it. Dandelions, I told whomever would listen, were only considered *weeds* because we didn't want them where they happened to be growing. "A rosebush in a dandelion field would be a weed," I proclaimed. And that's true enough. My sister Kathy gave me a bouquet of dandelions on my sixteenth birthday. I loved her for it because I knew that she was *not* mocking me.

A weed is any plant a member of the *homo sapien* clan considers ugly, unwanted, or troublesome. So a *wanted* weed isn't a weed at all. For those who enjoy dandelion greens as a nutritious addition to salads, dandelions are not weeds at all. Conversely, Mark calls the microgreens I grow every spring "weeds," reflecting his distaste for them more than any real flora categorization. So yes, much of this task of identifying weeds lies in the eye of the beholder.

But a weed can also be something that really, truly doesn't belong where it is growing. Some plants get brought into a place that doesn't have the particular nibblers or cold/hot, wet/dry climate that kept it in check wherever it originated. These non-native plants can crowd out native ones and wreak havoc on the natural habitat of a place. Take Himalayan blackberries in Oregon. The Oregon Department of Agriculture lists it as a noxious weed. It didn't originate here, but grows amazingly well, out competing *everything*. I'm fighting on behalf of native lady and sword ferns when I rip up blackberry vines down by the creek. When Mark hoes the garden, he fights on behalf of strawberries, beets, onions, and, yes, even zucchini, which many consider a weed of another sort.

So, when Caroline (one of the many visitors to come walk around Fern Creek) asked how we kept weeds so completely out of our vegetable gardens, berry patches, and orchard, I told her that in the spring, when vegetables are young and vulnerable, Mark spends about six hours a week hoeing. Later in the season three hours a week keeps chamomile, chickweed, thistle, and yes, dandelion from propagating in the gardens. The farmer's adage rings true—to spend less time weeding, one only has to keep up with the weeding. Partly the squash, cucumber, carrot, broccoli, tomato, and cabbage plants are big enough to compete with their competitors. Partly Mark designed the gardens so that we only water the vegetables and not the paths between raised beds and rows. Weeds can't grow well because they weren't allowed to develop deep roots back in the spring that would allow them to flourish during the dry spells.

But if Mark hung up his hoe and gloves, the weeds would make a quick comeback. Next spring after all those vegetable plants have died away, the weeds would be ready to reassert themselves in the garden. A weed-free garden takes tenacity, and that keeps us tenacious.

We divide and conquer. I concentrate on keeping various flowerbeds around Fern Creek free of weeds while Mark works in the gardens. This time of year my walk up the hill that used to start the day is more often spent working my way around the house, weeding a chunk at a time. It takes me seven to ten days to get all the way around, and then I start again—as Mark does in the gardens.

We are somewhat less tenacious when it comes to tackling several acres that we are transitioning from pasture to forest. In the absence of cows that once helped keep it all munched down, the field became a haven for Canada thistle, bull thistle, dock, tansy, and a few other noxious and ordinary weeds. We spend a couple of days in July walking through the now-adolescent forest (not yet big enough to offer serious competition to the weeds) with a black plastic bag in one hand and clippers in the other. Ours is a hot and thankless job. We clip blossoms and cut down plants, thankful that the two of us do this work side by side as it would be overwhelming for one of us alone. In the fall and again next spring, Mark will bring out the big guns and walk the field again, spraying each thistle with Roundup and Crossbow. Some plants require a fair bit of persistence if you don't want them to flourish.

All that to say Mark and I have learned to stay on top of our weeding to keep noxious things from taking root.

Is it too obvious to say we've noticed marriage presents the same challenge? After more than 30 years we still have to keep up with some weeding, pulling up non-natives that are crowding out what we're trying to cultivate. For instance, my tendency to micro manage has taken tenacious effort to eradicate. The result is quite satisfying. What we've been attempting to cultivate is doing well, growing strong, and out-competing most of the weeds. But the deepest-rooted ones, like Canada thistle, spread because they propagate underground, sending shoots out horizontally. Weeds like this take a special kind of attention—year-round attention with the hope that the root system will eventually shrivel up and decompose, starved of the nutrients necessary for it to keep cropping up.

Some plants, like Canada thistle, will be troublesome wherever they thrive, but after our years of marriage we're learning to accept and even enjoy that a less troublesome plant may be a flower to one of us, even if still perceived as a weed by the other. Dandelions might fare quite well in some fields, bringing more joy than sorrow to the flora and fauna residing there, and roses could, after all, be weeds in a field of clover hay.

Mark

Home Building

Outdoor sports, ballroom dancing, and local theater are lovely, and Lisa and I have done some of each of these together, but we're much more likely to be partnering around a pile of lumber. Some couples ski together; Lisa and I build chicken coops and hen houses.

I've enjoyed construction projects for years, then Lisa signed on in our late 40s when we built much of our own home on Fern Creek. There is something about pulling electrical wire with your spouse when your hands are numb from the cold that creates a strong bond of confidence and camaraderie. We finished the house, and now we just keep finding new things to build. These days we're building a hen house for the lower garden, knowing that chickens are about the best critters organic gardeners can have in the winter.

Building together can create some stress. Plans and details have to be negotiated, and that is not always easy, especially with two strong-minded people. But far more compelling than the occasional tension is the beautiful rhythm of teamwork we have learned.

Yesterday we covered two hen house walls with plywood which will later be gilded with lap siding (some people tell us that our hen houses look more like guest houses). Lisa and I carried the half-inch plywood from the pickup to the sawhorses, two sheets at a time, each carrying one end. I measured the length of the cut while she positioned the chalk snap line. I stretched the line tight. She snapped it. I cut the plywood while she held it, then I hoisted it up against the 2 x 4 walls while she put in the first nails. Then she finished nailing it as I started measuring the next piece. Though we didn't speak much (our ear protectors don't lend themselves to hearing anyway), we have learned to anticipate and communicate, with or without words. In less than an hour we installed six sheets of plywood. We were in the zone, just as we were the day we built an entire porch railing for our house's wraparound porch and the time we constructed oodles of crates for our CSA operation in a couple of hours.

Whenever we build together, I am struck by the metaphor. Building a house—or a hen house—is much like building a home. So what is required to build a home? At least these: persistence, humility, communication, and a sense of humor.

Pulling wire at 6 a.m. in an Oregon December had its rewards, but it also required a good deal of persistence and tenacity. Lisa and I learned about each other—that we are tough and resolved even as our glove-covered fingers stiffened with cold. We were a team, working together to get a job done well. We had done it before, not with copper wire, but with three lovely children. That, too, required some persistence, especially when we faced challenges during their adolescent years. These days we gather with our three daughters, their husbands and children, and feel a deep sense of blessing with our investment in their lives, as well as theirs in ours.

We were not perfect parents. In moments of candor, any of our daughters would be happy to speak of our strengths and our mistakes—and rightly so. Humility means we see ourselves clearly, including successes and foibles. Building a home is really just a sequence of errors punctuating a series of victories. As Lisa and I moved the new hen house door into place, I realized that I framed the opening three inches too short. I could have tried blaming someone (not sure who, since I measured for the door) or figured out some way to gerrymander a weird opening to the hen house, but the better choice was simply to admit my mistake and do what I could to fix it. It took an unpleasant hour of sawing and pounding and rebuilding, but eventually the door opening was the right size. I wish it were as simple to undo some of my parenting errors, but I think our children have appreciated our best efforts to do as well as we can as parents and to admit our mistakes.

Ear protectors make my already-compromised hearing quite dysfunctional. Lisa likes to talk when we build, so I nod a lot. Sometimes I actually hear her, but mostly I just nod. Still, communication is a huge part of our work together when we build. Sometimes it happens with words, sometimes with gestures or facial expression, and sometimes just with years of knowing each other that makes us anticipate what the other needs. Sometimes couples overemphasize communication, saying, "We have a communication problem," when the marriage is in shambles for other reasons. But communication really does matter. Building a home requires clear and meaningful speaking and our best efforts at listening. One of my most cherished memories of raising children is dinnertime. Almost every evening we sat around our old round table, five souls returning from our day's activities, pondering the big and small questions of life. If asked for my best suggestion about building a home, I would probably give two: eat dinner together, and talk while you're doing it.

Okay, maybe three words of advice: laugh. Find ways to keep humor in your home, to love life, to fill the evenings with hope and laughter. Life is brimming with good fun, with paradoxes and irony, with creativity and moments of frivolity. When our dining room light flickers, which it does a lot, Lisa and I smile and blame the electricians who wired our house on those cold December mornings.

CULTIVATING
FAITH AND
INTEGRITY

The Arms of God

On a sunny late February day, Mark and I were moving dirt for a construction project. That day was also only the second day we'd let the six-week-old pullets out of the hen house to get a taste of the world of grubs, bugs, grass, and greens that awaited them. Somewhere in the arch of a shovel full of dirt I tossed out of the excavation site, I saw unusual flurrying of wings among the pullets. They could fly that high, I supposed in that moment, but I doubted it. Sensing trouble I dropped the shovel and hightailed it up to the chicken yard in time to see a hawk fly up to one of the fence posts to wait out my visit. I waved my arms at her and like a very mad mother yelled, "No! No! No!"

She complied and flew off, but with a slowness that said, "You have not scared me one iota; I just find you annoying." I entered the yard and saw Amelia lying on the ground with a blood spot on her neck and the top of her head. Worse yet, her head lay bent at an unnatural angle, and she made no effort to move. I picked her up and she looked at me—grateful, I'd like to think.

The rest of the pullets had skedaddled inside for cover, so I shut the hen house door to give them a greater sense of safety, doubting they'd venture out again any time soon. Still, I *could* imagine that hawk flying right through their door and taking up where she left off.

Mark met me halfway back to the house, looked at Amelia dubiously and offered to put her down. I said, "But look, there's still so much life in her!" Her eyes were clear, her breathing normal. She looked *mostly* normal cupped in my hands.

But when I lay her in a box lined with pine shavings, she flopped into the same terrible position in which I'd found her on the ground, and I knew she was wounded beyond repair. So after some minutes, I turned her over to Mark and went back up to the coop to count the other pullets. I counted 13. We had 15. So I started counting out the breeds and discovered that Olivia, the other Amerucauna, was missing, and I grieved for her. Maybe the fear of the sky falling down had been bred out of these two to a greater degree, having ancestors that never actually *saw* the sky and therefore failed to fear things that swooped down from the sky upon them. Maybe that lack of instinct made her less skittish of a predator that should have terrified her. The hawk likely picked her off first and then came back for Amelia. Maybe a pair of hawks had come hunting.

Two days and two nights later (cold February days and nights), as I left the hen house after spending time with the pullets—feeding them and freshening their water—I heard a pullet chirp that sounded like it came from under the hen house. Sure enough, Olivia peeked out from under the hen house, looking skinnier and with ruffled feathers, desperate to get back to the fold but not eager for me pick her up and put her there. She didn't trust me—the big, hawk-like creature swooping down from above that I am.

So I set some food for her by the edge of the hen house and jogged down to the house to tell Mark the remarkable news that little Olivia had survived coyotes, foxes, cold weather, and a lack of easy food and water for 48 hours. We came back with brooms and a commitment to save this hardy little bird that wanted saving but couldn't cooperate with us for her own good. We prodded, poked, crawled, pleaded, bribed, and eventually, after several false attempts, I grabbed her when she trapped herself between the fence and me.

She calmed down as soon as I had her in my arms; glad enough, I reckon, to be caught.

I took her inside the hen house, unsure if the other pullets would welcome her back without punishing her for being gone, and she stayed in my lap for a minute, perhaps unsure of the same. But when Mark entered into the hen house it sent everybody scurrying, and she hid among them and found them welcoming and willing to embrace her back into the flock without question.

I wonder how often I am like that. Lost, desperate to be returned to the fold, yet afraid to let God catch me up and place me there. I don't know what I fear more—that God might crush me in the catching or that I will not be welcomed back.

May my children and grandchildren, students, colleagues, and friends learn that the world holds not only hawks looking for easy prey, but also those (God included) who are eager to protect and nurture. May I learn it, too. And may I learn that God never stops pursuing us, going to amazing lengths to gather us safely and take us home.

Mark

Finding God in the Pole Beans

Farming is for observant souls. Lisa and I make a pattern of walking the gardens in the evening, celebrating the growth fostered by the sunshine of the day while also looking for pests that may be feasting on the cabbage, fungi inhabiting the squash leafs, and the ever-persistent slugs that slosh around in the Oregon rain until they land on our lettuce. Our observations leads to various organic remedies for the problems we find and also to a daily ritual of celebrating the goodness of food. If we ever stop observing and responding, our crops will belong to critters. Occasionally, such relentless observation seems onerous, but more often it seems like discipline. And like most disciplines, observation easily becomes a spiritual discipline—a practice as likely to occur amidst the green beans as in the prayer chapel.

My daughter, Megan Anna Neff, and I enjoyed a nice conversation while picking beans in the upper garden. Grace (Megan Anna and Luke's two-month-old daughter) cooed contentedly in her Moby Wrap as Megan Anna and I filled our 5-gallon bucket with Blue Lake pole beans. Megan Anna, a recent seminary graduate, pondered aloud the upcoming adventure of teaching her first university class—a survey of the entire Bible for freshmen and sophomores. Our discussion drifted, as good conversations do, and soon we were talking about spiritual epiphanies.

Megan Anna took me to be jesting when I told her that some of my most powerful spiritual moments in recent years have come while picking green beans. Like most epiphanies, words of explanation fall short, but I gave it a try. There is something quite amazing about observing the rhythm of food production: tilling a parcel of land, adding some organic products of the earth to serve as fertilizer, planting a few small beans in the loose soil, weeding and watering, seeing sprouts turn into plants, and then finally harvesting pounds of beans. This rhythm, which occurs so faithfully that it might easily seem predictable or even boring, sometimes seeps around the edges of my goal-oriented existence and amazes me as a symbol of God's faithful presence in our world. The bean as symbol is important enough, but the real epiphany comes when I see that it is so much more than a symbol; it is also a bean. The bean itself—crisp, tender, delicious, nutritious—*is* God's grace, remarkable in its abundance, its earthiness, its practicality. God is surely present in the garden, giving life and hope.

Beans, like squash and tomatoes, bring me out of the ivory tower and back to earth. I love the life of the mind. My career is built around the world of ideas—comprehending them, expressing them to others, allowing my mind to imagine various dimensions and nuances of what others have written and spoken. And I especially love theology—thinking deeply about the ways God relates to us. This mental life, which so easily devolves into a Gnostic life, is where I spend most of my days. So seeing a green bean in the garden, and touching it, is the yin for my normal life's yang. In the garden I see a faint reflection of what encountering Jesus must have been—not the idea of Jesus, but the physical, tangible Word who became flesh and dwelled among us. It reminds me of that most famous Bible verse of all, that God so loved the world—not the idea of the world, or the potential of the world, or even just the people in the world, but the world itself and all it contains. It seems fair enough to say God loves green beans, too.

The present moment—each moment, really—is packed with so much grace. Grace in the Moby Wrap, in the eyes of my dear daughter as she talked about teaching her first class, in the 75-degree evening, the gentle breeze, the blue sky, the beans we picked. Grace is all around, just waiting to be noticed. How often I fail to notice the moment, thinking instead about what has to be done today or later this week, or before I retire. But this moment, this glorious moment, contains so much to be observed and celebrated.

God, help me notice.

On Thankfulness for Old Barns and Old Farmers

We're about ready to re-route the hens from their summer yard into the upper garden, giving them access to vegetables nearing the end of the growing season. The chickens will munch down bean, zucchini, cucumber, and tomato plants; fertilize; eat grubs; scratch up the weeds; and work in compost. The garden will be a gift to the chickens and their winter stay will nurture the dirt that has produced faithfully for us this season.

Re-routing involves crafting a run of sorts from the hen house to a place we cut open in the garden fence. It's about a six-foot span, and since I am constructing the run, it will look homemade but be functional. *Homemade* means I will construct it out of whatever materials I can scrounge up.

I found leftover fencing in the shop, but needed a plank to help the hens exit and enter the hen house.

Whenever I'm in need of an odd piece of lumber or a crate or a burlap bag, I head to the deserted barn next door where a farmer dried hazelnuts years ago. *I think I am redeeming something already decaying and doomed for the dump as soon as the property on which it sits is sold.* Mark is pretty sure I am stealing.

On that sunny late October day, I took my cross-country path through the woods to the barn. I hadn't visited since March when I waded through wild daffodils bumping up through a thick ivy groundcover where sunlight hit the slope near the barn. A rusting orange piece of farm equipment marked the entrance and I stopped to breathe in the familiar musty air. I picked my way through the barn, letting my eyes adjust to the dark. At the far end the fall sun splashed through a broken door, falling on two old tires, a can of rusty nails, a box of screws and nuts, a pile of ancient hazelnut shells, and a most magnificent spider web.

I found a plank that would do nicely and then high-tailed it home so I could return with my camera before the sun moved on. As I snapped pictures I thought of the lives lived out here before when the plowed field, now for sale, nurtured a hazelnut orchard, and a family made their livelihood growing and drying their own and other local farmers' hazelnuts. I wonder if they sat by the creek the way I do and listened to it tumble downstream, if they loved this land and all it holds and nurtures as much as I do.

I went upstairs where the bats live and walked into what was once an office. Again I considered redeeming the high-backed double bench and desk, then again heard Mark's voice in my head, sighed, and figured that whoever buys this place may find some value in those pieces. I hope so.

A sense of goodness draws around me in that barn. Part of the goodness is simple appreciation for the people who faithfully spent their lives tending the land. They kept the orchards healthy even as they knew wealth would not come to them through hazelnuts.

I am thankful that God created an earth that renews itself, is adaptable, and can heal from wounds. What was once forest could be replaced by an orchard, which may someday become a vineyard or perhaps a 25-acre diverse small farm. Fern Creek times five.

I hope the barn stays around for a long while. It would make a lovely gathering place with a bit of refurbishing. At this, Mark chuckles, though not unkindly. The west wall has crumbled and with it a good portion of the roof. One enters at one's own risk. But the barn, even as it is, remains beautiful to me—a reminder of those who cared for this land, grew food, and etched out a life on this rural hillside a number of years ago. I feel an inexplicable thankfulness to them for carrying on the tradition of growing the next generation, and for growing food and building barns and living with an awareness of our need for healthy dirt, good water, fresh air.

Even now, a generation or so later, I take delight in the hillside of daffodils that spring forth anew every March; in the nearby springhouse and its accompanying spring that flows year after year, supplying the creek that gives Fern Creek half its name; and in the bats that have made the barn their home in these latter years. I want to preserve this place where there are lessons to be learned, poetry to be found.

Mark

Life and Death

I'm not sure why we name our chickens, but I'm sure it has more to do with Lisa than with me. It gets confusing when we have two or three chickens that look *exactly* the same, but have different names. Lisa somehow notices the nuances. "Greta has a lighter comb than Liesel," she'll say. Or, "Sule has a crooked toe."

I look again. "Really?"

Even if I see no difference, I do my best to learn chicken names anyway, feeling convinced that being a good farmer and a good husband demands nothing less. This story is about Liesel, who may have once been Greta, who looks a lot like Penelope, who reminds me of Sule with the crooked toe.

It was going to be a great essay. We found Liesel drooling in the grass one hot July day, looking like she was about to die. Lisa and I pondered our options. As I headed into the house to change into slaughtering clothes to do my least favorite thing about farming, Lisa stopped me for a conversation about our options. We decided to let Liesel die a natural death rather than euthanizing her. (*Euthanizing* is a euphemism for cutting a chicken's head off, which I have only done a few times, each of them terrible.)

We created a little fenced area that we called the infirmary, filled an extra chicken waterer with some hen medicine we found at our farm supply store, and then watched to our amazement as Liesel drank and drank the medicine. On death's door, she was fighting to live. The next day she looked better, drank more medicine, and even ate a little chicken food. I started forming the essay in my head about how thoroughly creation heals and how God's redemptive presence can be found everywhere we look. Where, O death, is your sting?

Less than a week later, I was digging Leisel's grave before filling it with her lifeless body, a couple feet of dirt, and my idea for an essay. It took about five days for her to die. Leisel never appeared to be in misery, though I suppose there is always some inherent misery in dying, however invisible it may be to those who live on.

The essay would have been inspiring if Leisel had lived. Her story would have borne some faint resemblance to the time I thought I buried our family cat, but discovered a couple weeks later—when Friskie came bouncing home—that I had buried the wrong cat. But not every story can be about life. We all must stare at death from time to time in order to remember what it means to live. Though I am sad about Leisel's plight, I think by dying she gave me a more important essay to write.

I wonder how often we euphemize dying. Just to be clear, I've moved on from chickens and am thinking about those terrible times when a fellow human dies. We call it *passing away*, reassure ourselves about the hope of heaven, and tell one another that our diseased friend is now in a happier place. Death has no sting. In the process of sanitizing the whole thing, I wonder if we fail to grasp the outrageous tragedy of death.

Don't get me wrong. I believe in heaven. C. S. Lewis observed that if we throw out the idea of heaven, then we have to throw out all of Christianity. But sometimes we seem to say that death is better than life. "We're just passing through," we tell ourselves, on our way to our heavenly home. We may even quote a few verses from the eleventh chapter of Hebrews about being sojourners and pilgrims on earth, believing we have represented God well by minimizing the tragedy of death.

We forget Jesus sweating blood in Gethsemane.

We forget that all creation groans for freedom from death.

We forget Jesus weeping in empathy when Lazarus was lying in a tomb.

Perhaps we can't fully understand the goodness of *this* life if we don't fully understand the tragedy of it ending. God created the earth—and humans on the earth—and called it good. If God were inclined to the triviality of bumper stickers, perhaps God's first bumper sticker would have been: "Life Is Good."

Breathe. Smell. Listen. Look. Touch. All around us is the fullness of life; all of it revealing something grand about our gracious Creator. Christianity is a tangible, earthy faith, made visible by the incarnation.

Paradoxically, we know the goodness of life, in part, through witnessing its loss. The vast majority of the 2,423,712 U.S. deaths in a typical year will leave relatives and friends in the midst of the crashing and sometimes crushing waves of grief. Sensations of losing one we love, coupled with the existential angst of knowing our own life on earth is fleeting, bear witness to our intrinsic awareness that life is worth living.

Handling death in the stiff body of a chicken reminded me of the distastefulness and outrageousness of death, even for a critter we call fowl. And how much more awful it is when a husband or wife, a brother or sister, a father or mother, a daughter or son dies. Or when we face our own death. I am past the two-thirds point on this journey toward death, which is now expected to occur when I reach 77.9 years. Wednesday, May 13, 2037, is looking like a bad day. If death brings deep pangs of sorrow and grief, if it penetrates like a dagger, and if it wounds like that dagger being turned and twisted, then I think somehow we have it right.

Death stings for a reason. The reason is life—full, deep, abundant life that brings laughter and love and eventually the wrinkles that bear witness to the blessed years we have been granted. As long as we breathe, we breathe in the redeeming grace of God who created us to experience this good life.

Lisa

Choosing Paths

For our birthdays Rae and Aubry gave Mark and me a membership to the Japanese Gardens in Portland. We're caring for our granddaughter Juniper on Mondays this sabbatical year, and they thought (rightly so) that we might enjoy seasonal jaunts to the gardens as an enticement for driving the 30 miles from Fern Creek to Portland each week.

My dear friend Marcile joined me for my inaugural visit.

We walked through an old authentic Japanese Gate, a gift from Japan. I marvel sometimes at how quickly these two powerful nations became diplomatic friends after being such horrible enemies not so long ago. The path from the gate led uphill through dense woods, each step taking us into a deeper green quiet. I showed my card at the official entrance and saw that we had arrived early enough to walk in the contemplative quiet offered to "members only."

Once in the gardens we followed paths that meandered across footbridges, by a traditional tea room, rock gardens, and ponds. A couple of times we stood still and listened to the different water sounds that we could hear all at once—the creek bubbling along the path, the waterfall in the not-too-distant distance, and the drip of water falling from a bamboo pipe into a stone basin. It is timed so that a drop hits the surface just after the last ripple has smoothed away. Trees arched and turned their branches this way and that, creating a canopy of leaves that let dappled shade spill onto the growing moss canvas at our feet. Textures and shades, shadows, and the sounds of water called us to a gentle sort of attention.

Eventually we sat on a bench in one of the gazebos, resting on individual woven rattan squares inset into the wooden bench. We talked about a friend of Marcile's, now in hospice care and awaiting death, and some friends and family members newly struggling to adapt to hard life changes. We sat side by side thankful for life, health, and friendship; aware of the precarious nature of gentle, calm seasons such as we were both living.

After some quiet Marcile said, "I understand that everything in Japanese gardens is done with purpose. What do you suppose is the purpose for the different stones used in the path coming and going to this bench?" I let my eyes follow hers and saw that irregular shaped gray stones led to our bench and that our feet rested on a long rectangle-shaped white slab—maybe made from concrete, maybe cut from a large, once irregular stone. At the far end of the bench the slab ended and another irregular stone served the feet of the weary traveler who chose to sit there. Leaving the bench, one could take irregular shaped stones back to the main path or choose the first two steps to be on the smooth rectangle slab before stepping onto a gravel path.

"What do you think they might mean?" I asked because I had no idea what purpose any of that might serve, not having noted the varying stones until Marcile pointed them out.

"Maybe the stones are laid out this way to welcome travelers as they come—with rumpled, scattered, maybe heart-broken lives. You come here and sit and perhaps find some peace. Maybe you notice life and loveliness and feel a bit more grounded as you leave. But," and here she nodded at the irregular stone at the end of the bench, "maybe you don't come wanting or expecting or feeling capable of hope, but come to sit for a spell anyway."

"And when we leave," I suggested, entering her wonderment, "we might not feel we have done more than sit with our chaos and burden, and leave the way we came, but maybe we can leave by a calmer road because we have remembered some beauty, or that some good lies beyond this bad moment. Or maybe we simply remember God loves us and let ourselves be renewed by that."

Current hard moments fail to define what is possible in the future, even when the hard moments are as ugly as Pearl Harbor and Hiroshima. We can choose to forgive, make peace, embrace, to plant and cultivate with the hope of harvest. Every moment holds the opportunity to be open to love and loveliness.

As we left the gazebo we walked up steps that blended rough-hewn stone and smooth, ordered slabs. Nearing the top of the stairs they all became ordered slabs and I said, "And maybe this shift to smooth slabs represents the hope that as we near life's end we have accepted what is and are ready to accept what is to come." Marcile nodded. "For the Shinto that would look different than for the Christian." She murmured agreement.

I am blessed by this dear friend who observes life fully and has walked a long obedience in the same direction for more than 70 years. She is 20 years ahead of me and has not only been my friend for more than 20 years, but also a model for who I want to become. I met her when she was younger than I am now, newly widowed and working in the church Mark and I chose to attend after moving to Newberg.

We talk about vocation ("You are not your vocation, Lisa," she reminds me as I contemplate leaving it to make time for other things and wonder what changes it would bring to my identity). We talk about faith, doubt, forgiveness, grace, gardening, baking, books, tattoos, grandparenting, and marriage.

Marcile pays attention to life and loves and affirms it all. She inspires me to do the same.

Mark

A Magnificat Moment

I find myself attentive to *moments* these days. Little events that once would have skimmed the surface of my consciousness now settle in with gravity and rich meaning. Yesterday's moment occurred during Sunday morning worship at Newberg Friends Church.

I don't always love the Advent season. We have lost Christmas to the marketers of the world, which makes me grumpy, and I sometimes even take my holiday grumpiness to church where it doesn't belong. But yesterday's moment broke through my resistance as our pastor, Gregg, asked the women in the gathering to read the Magnificat aloud. The Magnificat (also known as the "Song of Mary") is found in the Gospel of Luke, where Mary expresses her wonder and awe that God would choose her to help change the world.

In itself, this could have been a forgettable Advent moment. We often do congregational readings, and with

Christmas approaching the Magnificat seems a reasonable choice. But yesterday the voice emerging from a community of women all around me sank deep into my soul, causing me to reflect and ponder and miss a bit of Gregg's sermon.

The Magnificat is a prayer of strength. It pronounces the importance of a woman—of all women, really—while honoring a God who is not overly impressed with wealth or prestige or any of the typical markers of success.

The voice I heard most clearly was the one immediately to my left, owned by the woman who has been my partner for all these years. "Oh, how my soul praises the Lord. How my spirit rejoices in God my Savior!" Faith hasn't always been easy for Lisa. One cannot get a PhD in sociology without having hard questions raised about world religions. Lisa's childhood faith has been stirred considerably by her education, and yet she holds tenaciously to what she believes is true. At one time she believed it with 100 percent of her brain, and now she estimates her cortical belief to be at 92 percent, but that's plenty for her to be a whole-hearted believer who shapes her core values and makes important life decisions consistent with her faith values. I love her resilience.

Then my thoughts left the church and settled on our small farm. I pondered Lisa using power tools, shoveling and hoeing and raking, carrying 60-pound bags of concrete mix, cleaning the occasional chicken that we have to kill, driving our little John Deere, helping move firewood—even cutting it with the chainsaw sometimes. All these are images of strength—inner and outer fortitude that shape Lisa's character.

In our Protestant tradition we often minimize the role of Mary in saving the world. The Magnificat reminds me of

Mary's central role in God's drama. What a counter cultural, radical thing for this poor young girl to be chosen to carry and birth the Messiah.

> For he took notice of his lowly servant girl,
> and from now on all generations will call me blessed.
> For the Mighty One is holy,
> and he has done great things for me.
>
> (Luke 1:48-49, *New Living Translation*)

What strength it must have taken to face a scoffing world that questioned the circumstances of her pregnancy—and still questions today—to stand and worship God rather than shrink in shame.

My thoughts wandered beyond Lisa to the chorus of women reciting the Magnificat. For a moment it seemed to echo through all the ages—women speaking the voice of Mary, the voice of power and importance and strength; women who have been enslaved and objectified and abused; women who have been educated and empowered and ordained and elected to office. I heard all women speaking together in one voice, speaking words of praise to God for turning the power structures of the world upside down.

> He shows mercy from generation to generation
> to all who fear him.
> His mighty arm has done tremendous things!
> He has scattered the proud and haughty ones.
> He has brought down princes from their thrones
> and exalted the humble.
> He has filled the hungry with good things
> and sent the rich away with empty hands.
>
> (Luke 1:50-53, *New Living Translation*)

These are the moments that renew my faith, moments that remind me that these deeply held beliefs are much bigger than who goes to heaven. No, this is a faith for today—for here and now—and a faith for the ages. It is a countercultural thing, a radical wonder that turns power structures upside down and has done so since the moment of its conception. This faith brings me back to the Christmas lost to the marketers; to Christ's call to pursue truth, grace, justice, and compassion with every remaining day of my life. This faith brings me back to sing alongside Mary and Lisa.

Lisa

On Preservation

Wednesday and Saturday mornings during the summer and fall we harvest whatever is ripe and ready for our CSA. Each of these afternoons, families that support our farming endeavor come to Fern Creek to pick up a crate of food. By early August the crates are filled with yellow and green and purple beans, zucchini, yellow and tromboncini squash, raspberries or strawberries, kale or chard, broccoli, cucumbers, corn, onions, and tomatoes. Sometimes I add something extra—a few lavender shortbread cookies along with lavender and the recipe, or zucchini yeast rolls, or a jar of freshly harvested honey.

After we fill the crates we see what is left over and always abundance surrounds us. Some of the extra we offer to our CSA families, some we offer our hens (mostly the rumpled or overly mature produce), and some we preserve.

As of today—the last week in August—our pantry holds 34 quarts of beans, a dozen pints of pickled beets, and 13 quarts of pickles. Pesto cubes frozen in ice cube trays are stored in the freezer along with gallon-size bags of snap and snow peas and berries. We've dehydrated strawberries and blueberries and dried herbs in bunches hanging them on a string in the kitchen. Onions and garlic hang in clusters in the workshop where potatoes are drying on racks. Tomatoes and apples are still ahead of us.

Mostly Mark and I do the preserving work together. Mark prefers bean snapping. He can mindlessly stand near the sink snapping the ends off beans while I ready the jars, get the pressure cooker heating up, fill the jars, and then load the canner.

Preserving food has a long and rich history. Once folks settled down and stopped following their food around (as in elk and ripening berries), they started finding ways to store and preserve it during seasons when it didn't grow so plentifully out of the ground. People dried, pickled, and salted meats and vegetables, and turned milk into cheese and grapes into wine (preservation of a fairly different sort). Advances in science and agriculture in the eighteenth and nineteenth century took food preservation out of the family kitchen and storage out of the root cellar, moving the process into factories that canned, milled grains, slaughtered animals, and made our cheeses. A lot of people could be fed on the science and industry of the eighteenth and nineteenth century, and at the time people felt like we (as in, individuals) hadn't lost any skills or knowledge worth, well, *preserving*.

I wonder what it suggests that a word we use to talk about making food fit to eat later (preservation) primarily refers to keeping something safe—such as a forest, or a way of life, or to keep something from destruction or decay (like a Rembrandt painting, the Declaration of Independence, or a wedding gown). Maybe it suggests that anything worthwhile needs some sort of preservation—whether to ensure we can use it later, or because it has inherent value and needs to be protected from that which might mindlessly, or intentionally, destroy it.

So yes, we preserve food to make it safe from botulism or rot, but we also preserve it so that it will nourish us well later. And in so doing we preserve some old way of living as well. Come January we'll open a jar of beans or make a fruit cobbler from frozen berries, and a satisfaction will settle over the dining room table and fill our stomachs.

Preservation reminds me how dependent I am on things outside myself that need varying levels of preserving. I receive energy from much that has been preserved: food from the land when it seemingly slumbers, relationships that have been nurtured for decades, and skills passed down to me from my mothers. I depend on these energy resources in order to teach, write, build gazebos and bridges; to tend grandchildren, students, chickens, bees, and my very dear husband.

While food preservation may not be particularly difficult, one still has to learn the art. Each of our daughters came to Fern Creek this season to preserve food. I like to think old learning is being rediscovered in wisdom passing from one generation to the next.

Trial and error is also a good teacher—it taught me not to use overly mature beans in my jars, how to walk alongside my adolescent daughters, and how to better love my husband. But much of what I've learned—probably *most* of what I've learned—has come from others as a gift of preservation. My mother and mother-in-law have been some of my great teachers, along with dear friends—both peers and those a bit farther along in life's journey—who have preserved important things well over the years and so have been able to draw sustenance in seasons when the land rests under cold days and darkness falls early.

Mark

On Earth As It Is in Heaven

Jonathan Edwards, the great American theologian who, sadly enough, may be best known for his sermon "Sinners in the Hands of an Angry God," delivered an amazing sermon about heaven in 1738. He titled it "Heaven Is a World of Love." Throughout his sermon, Edwards used images of water to demonstrate the abundance of heaven and the purity of love we will experience there.

> There in heaven this fountain of love, this eternal three in one, is set open without any obstacle to hinder access to it. There this glorious God is manifested and shines forth in full glory, in beams of love; there the fountain overflows in streams and rivers of love and delight, enough for all to drink at, and to swim in, yea, so as to overflow the world as it were with a deluge of love.
> (Jonathan Edwards, *The Sermons of Jonathan Edwards: A Reader*, Yale University Press, 1999, p. 245).

FAITH & INTEGRITY

Since first reading this sermon ten years ago on the advice of a psychotherapy client, I have come back to this image over and over: a God who delights in pouring out blessings in what Edwards called a "deluge of love." Heaven and earth may be quite different, but not utterly different. Life on this earth is filled with its own blessings, God's outpouring of love, God's kingdom here and now.

Last August and September Lisa and I faced a sort of problem as our gardens produced far more than we imagined possible. Each week we loaded up the crates for the families subscribing to our CSA, made additional piles of extra food for any surplus they might want, gave away food to department colleagues, and still had more than we could manage—onions and beets and cabbage and tomatoes and squash and corn overflowing. It seemed so clearly a deluge of God's love.

Lately I've experienced a growing awareness of God's love. Most days I feel absolutely overwhelmed by the deluge of God's blessings in life—pouring out, overflowing, on earth as it is in heaven. Life has been difficult at times, as every life is, but mostly I marvel at how very good life on this earth can be.

Blessings have deep roots. The longest blessing in my life is knowing my mother, being held first in her arms and then in her prayers, receiving her generosity and grace. She is a remarkable woman by any accounting, and I feel grateful for her guidance through my formative years. Now approaching 78 years old, she showed up this week to help us hoe in the garden—not because she doesn't have her own work to do but because she is a soul who thrives in her generosity, as do others who benefit from it.

Mom brought her own hoe with her—one with a special blade crafted by my grandfather in that old shop on his

Hillside farm that I used to love visiting. Loyd Anderson must have been a mechanical genius considering the things he made over his lifetime, yet this simple hoe my mother carried with her reminded me of how blessings flow down from one generation to another. The sins of the father follow us surely enough, but so do the blessings of a father, a mother, a grandparent. They wash over us time and time again, sometimes years after an ancestor has departed from this earthly existence. Loyd married Irene, a remarkable woman who died much too young. Still, in those 12 years when my life overlapped with Irene's, I learned what it means to be securely wrapped in the love of a grandparent. Loyd and Irene raised Donna—a farm girl with a work ethic that won't quit and the generous soul who became my mother.

Five years ago Mom showed up with a stainless steel shovel on a rainy February day to help us plant Douglas Fir trees. It looked brand new, but it was once Loyd's shovel, too. I observed how carefully my mother washed the shovel after using it to plant conifers in the red dirt we have at Fern Creek. It occurred to me that washing tools is a discipline for longevity. Water came from the outdoor spigot, pouring out on earth as it is in heaven—abundant, cleansing, keeping tools useful for generations to come.

My generation is vulnerable to a disposability myth. It seems anything can be replaced. I pick up a new hoe at Home Depot every couple of years. Beyond the tool itself, I wonder what I lose every time I discard an old broken tool and replace it with another shining specimen. Is there some part of me that gets lost along with those old tools? Seeing my mother with her old hoe and shovel, sharp as can be, used for years, built and used by my grandfather, reminds me that some blessings are strands through time, reaching from one generation into the next, bringing memories and cause for grateful reflection.

There will come a day when my mother departs this earth, as her mother before her. The hoe with that special blade crafted by my grandfather will be here still, as will the stainless steel shovel. If Lisa and I are still around, we will inherit those tools, and—rightly—we will cherish them. They will be daily reminders of God's blessings, overflowing throughout all creation, throughout all time, and beyond.

www.ingramcontent.com/pod-product-compliance
Lightning Source LLC
Chambersburg PA
CBHW062212080426
42734CB00010B/1863